MY LIFE AS A BANKER

A LIFE WORTH LIVING

"Find the Courage to go on, never giving up, even when the road of life curves."

AUTHOR BRENDA MOHAMMED

Contents

FOREWORD

"It is true of men and of watches, you may tell them by their works."

To have been asked to write the Foreword for the book, **My Life as a Banker: A Life Worth Living,** is an honour that will forever be etched in my memory.

Mrs. Brenda Mohammed, an award-winning author, has, without a doubt, shown through her writings the exemplary quality of her life. Her Christian upbringing has instilled in her a strong belief in God, who has guided her life from infancy. This is the true story of Brenda's life as a child, a teenager, a young adult, a wife, a mother, and a professional. Her achievements as both a mother and a professional are remarkable.

This book is an encouragement and example to all women.

It shows clearly what the power of God can do in someone's life.

By reading this book, we will learn something to enhance our own lives. The book stimulates us and encourages us to emulate the successes of the author. It touches our emotions and gives us a new appreciation of life. It encourages us to go on, never giving up, even when the road of life curves.

The author who is my younger sister, my friend, and my confidante is a kind, generous, caring and loving person and within the pages of her book, all women can find something with which to identify or emulate. This most significant autobiographical account of her life is worth reading.

It teaches us that with God in our lives, all things are possible, and all things work for good. It stimulates our power of thought and urges us on to greater heights.

This journey of her life leads us through prayer, joy, pain, and sorrow. She has fulfilled almost all her dreams despite challenges along the way.

Brenda's mark of excellence is stamped on her writings and on her life. I have witnessed her admirable lifestyle unfold before my eyes, and I have supported and stood by her all these years.

Brenda has also written a sequel to My Life as a Banker: A Life Worth Living. When you have finished reading this book, read **Retirement is Fun**. It is a whirlwind account of her life after retirement, and I recommend it.

Florabelle Lutchman – Retired School Principal

EARLY CHILDHOOD

What is a life worth living? To me, life begins with family and ends with family. I believe the love of a family is life's greatest gift. I was born into a wonderful family. Their love and support molded me into the person I would become.

My parents were Dr. and Mrs. Andrew M. Khan. My father was an Educator, and my mother was a needlework teacher. I was born at the time my father took up an appointment in Union Village, Claxton Bay, as the school's Head Master.

Union Village in the oil-rich Caribbean island of Trinidad was not yet a town. It was in proximity to the Texaco oil refinery. There were few retail businesses, and they were like small shops and parlours.

Houses were in no way majestic. My father's car was the only one in the village, and everyone knew when he was driving by.

The school and the Presbyterian Church were in the same compound with the headmaster's house. A huge almond tree stood majestically in the middle of the yard. My sisters and I played many games under that tree and feasted on the big, juicy almonds it bore. There was a large orchard of fruit trees at the back of the house. We enjoyed oranges, bananas, pomcytres, and mangoes whenever they were in season.

I had six sisters and three brothers. My parents told me that when I was born, two Canadian missionaries, a husband and wife who could not have children, approached my parents to adopt me. The husband was the Church Minister, and he had baptized me. They returned to Canada after one year in Trinidad.

I was the eighth child, and maybe they felt my parents would have willingly given me away to them.

My parents refused and they had two more girls after me.

I sometimes wonder what my life would have been like if my parents had agreed to give me to those Canadian Missionaries. I do not like to live in cold places and I dislike snow, so I would have been very lonely and unhappy in Canada without my brothers and sisters.

Do you believe there was no electricity in those days? Every evening at six o' clock, my mother lit the oil lamps so we could do our school homework. By seven o'clock or seven-thirty, I was fast asleep.

The house we lived in, although comfortable, was dreary looking as I recall. As we had no electricity and no refrigerator, my mother reared chickens at the side of the house for our meat supplies. When it rained, that area was very slimy. I fell down there many times.

My mother was a very creative person. She cared for us, sewed all of our clothes, did exquisite embroidery and crocheting, cooked delicious meals, and baked tasty treats for us. She often baked several loaves of bread and dozens of cakes in a primitive oven, which she constructed herself.

The aroma of freshly baked bread and cakes always permeated the entire house and projected a feeling of love and warmth in our home.

Not far away from the orchard at the back of the house, a river ran by, and my brothers took us fishing there many times. Sometimes they caught several fish and took them home for my mother to cook.

My father was very engrossed in his teaching career. In those days, education was not a priority for most people, and he sought to change that. He was always out visiting parents and encouraging them to send their children to school. One of his priorities was forming village committees to educate parents.

He was a staunch Presbyterian and believed in God and the power of prayer. Every Sunday, he took us to church. On evenings, he gathered the family together for family prayers.

Knowing how much we loved animals, my father bought two stark white lambs as pets for my elder sister and me. We named them Larry and Lana. We loved tending and taking them out on mornings to the orchards to feed on grass. They were very playful and loving.

One evening, when we went to bring them home, we found both lambs lying dead on the compost heap. We were heartbroken and ran home crying to tell our parents. They could not determine the cause of their sudden death, and after comforting us, arranged to bury them in a corner of the orchard. That was my first death experience.

In my father's spare time, he would take the whole family to the beach. At one time, he took us to Manzanilla, one of the popular beach resorts in Trinidad.

My sisters were sitting on a floating log, and I attempted to sit on it next to them. I slipped, fell off, and a huge wave swiftly carried me away. I knew I was drowning and heard my sisters screaming for my father to help me.

My father was also in the sea and he heard my sisters. He instantly swam across to save me. Luckily, I had long hair, to which he held on to gently pull me up. My father saved my life. I could always depend on him when I needed him.

My eldest sister was often away from home studying. When she came home, she helped my mother cook and bake. She was an excellent cook, and I enjoyed the meals she cooked. Once she took one of my sisters and me on the train to Tunapuna, which was a town many miles away from our home, to attend a function at her school.

From her school, we went on a trip to Blue Basin Waterfalls, a scenic place in a secluded valley surrounded by towering mountains in the north of Trinidad. It is one of the many tourist attractions in Trinidad. We did a great amount of walking to get there, and it took a long while to catch up with my sisters' friends.

For each of her siblings' birthdays, my sister baked lovely cakes and decorated them beautifully. She always loved to celebrate our birthdays with ice cream and cake.

Whenever I needed help, I called on another of my elder sisters. I could not pronounce her name when I was young and used to call her 'Billy'. She possessed a rare beauty and a sweet disposition. She always found time to look after me when my eldest sister or mother was not available.

I attended elementary school at the age of three. My father was the Head Teacher at the same school. I refused to stay in my class. I searched every class until I found my older sister who was in a higher class than mine, and I sat down next to her.

Her teacher said I could stay in her class provided I could cope with her teaching. Since I wanted to stay with my sister, I listened very attentively and learned everything that the teacher taught. When the teacher asked questions, I was the first to raise my hand. She was very impressed with my learning ability and promoted me to that class.

I took part in several school concerts, speaking contests, reciting poems, singing, and dancing competitions.

The teachers in the school remarked on my brilliance and learning aptitude.

When I was seven years old, my father received a promotion as Head Master of a bigger school in another district. It was a big change for me, moving from one village to the next. It was a much brighter area than Union Village, and I liked it. There was a popular cinema also, and my older sister, Myrtle, promised to take us to see movies.

We lived in the Head Master's quarters, and there was electricity in that house.

My father bought a large refrigerator and my mother stocked it with meats and goodies. She no longer had to rear chickens, and I was relieved since the yard was not messy and slimy as in our former residence. The church and school were in the same compound, similar to our previous home, and I liked the location change.

I attended the school there. Because of my age, I was placed in a lower class than my sister. When the teacher taught and asked questions, I answered them all correctly.

She was amazed, and after a couple weeks, she promoted me to my sister's class.

My new class was for students writing the Government Exhibition examinations the following year.

At eight years old, my teacher allowed me to write the examinations together with the older children as a practice test. I did not win a Government Exhibition at that age, but my name appeared in the newspapers among the passes.

My teacher found that I did quite well for my age and groomed me to win a college exhibition in the following year, when I would have been nine years old.

Around that time, one of my nieces. Ramona came to live with us since her mother had gone to Venezuela to live.

She was very pretty, and she was about the same age as my youngest sister. She was the daughter of my oldest brother. We loved her very much. We were very disappointed when her grandmother came and took her away.

One Saturday afternoon, I was in the bedroom, lying on the bed, looking after my youngest sister, Arabella. Being the baby in the family, everyone loved Susie. [her nickname] She was always allowed to have her way. She was about two and a half years old, and she was asleep. My mother had closed the window.

Suddenly, she awoke and stood on the bed, opened the window, and began jumping up and down. I closed the window and told her it was safer to keep it closed since the bed was high and she could fall through the window. She kept re-opening the window and kept jumping. I kept on closing the window and tried to call out to my mother to speak to her. My mother was in the kitchen and could not hear me.

I closed the window securely and left the room to fetch my mother. Just as I left the room, I heard one of my sisters who was downstairs screaming and saying that our baby sister had fallen out of the window. Everyone rushed downstairs and saw her lying on the grass. My eldest sister, my mother, and my father rushed her to the doctor. Not a bone was broken. She only received a slight cut close to her temple. It was a miracle.

I thought God himself must have reached out and helped her to land safely from the fall from that high house. She admitted that when I left the room, she reopened the window and jumped on the bed. She swore she would never do that again. In spite of that fall, Arabella, obtained her doctorate in Spanish in Buffalo, New York, and is a Spanish Professor at a college in Los Angeles, California.

I turned nine on 1st December that year and was preparing to write the Government College Exhibition

Examination together with my sister the following year. I was a member of the Junior Red Cross Society. We were required to visit a school further in the south to march with other members from other schools two days before the College Exhibition examination in June. My mother bought me a new pair of shoes to wear for the occasion. It cut the back of my right heel, and the following day, it pained me so much that I could not attend school.

My father and others left to go to school and work, and my mother told me to lie down and rest. She went downstairs to do her housework.

The school was in the same compound as our home, so everyone came home for lunch.

In the middle of the morning, I felt a pain in my right side but ignored it for a while. It became more intense, and by lunchtime, I was crying with pain.

When my father came home for lunch, he entered the bedroom to inquire how I was feeling. He saw me crying and thought my foot was hurting. When I told him that the pain was on my right side, he was surprised and concerned. He called out to my mother to get me dressed to take me to the doctor in San Fernando.

My mother was confused, as I had stayed home because of the pain in my foot. She left everything she was doing and helped me get dressed and took me to the car. She accompanied us to the doctor.

My father was very careful in his driving. He kept telling me that if he was driving too roughly, to tell him, and he would slow down because he did not want to aggravate my pain.

It seemed like hours before we got to the doctor's office. He saw me right away. When he examined me, he said I was suffering from acute appendicitis. I needed an emergency operation, failing which my appendix would rupture, causing my instant death.

He gave my father a letter to take to the San Fernando General Hospital. As soon as we arrived, the doctor on duty again examined me and confirmed that I needed emergency surgery. He told my father it was a matter of life and death.

The nurses prepared me for emergency surgery and wheeled me into the operating theatre on a stretcher. There I saw several doctors and nurses in white gowns waiting for me.

They placed me under a large light and gave me an anesthetic to make me sleep. I felt as if I was sailing down a large tunnel with a light at the end, and I heard loud laughter, then nothing.

When I awoke, I was in the ward with lots of other children, and my parents were standing next to my bed, sobbing. They were relieved when I opened my eyes. My mother said they saw the wardsmen bringing in my limp body from the operating room, and they thought I had died.

They both stayed with me for a long while. They did not leave the hospital until midnight.

The next day, all the students who wrote the Government Exhibition Examinations came to visit me after they wrote the exams. They brought ice cream, nuts, sweets, and other goodies, but I had no appetite to eat anything. The other children in the ward benefited from those delicacies.

The doctor discharged me from the hospital after a week. My right side, where the doctor had cut me, hurt, and I could not walk properly. I walked with a twist on my right side. I could not return to school for the rest of the term and spent the whole of the summer holidays recuperating.

When the Examiners released the results of the examination, my sister, Florabelle, won a Government exhibition, which made her eligible to attend Naparima Girls' High School in January of the following year.

It was back to elementary school for me, but I was still young. I was only nine years old and had many chances to write the exam. My class had a new teacher, and he taught us well.

I joined the school choir under the leadership of a lovely young teacher whom I admired. She taught us many melodious songs, and I gained a love for singing. I still remember many of the songs I learned from her to this day.

Another teacher trained a few of us to dance for a school concert. I recall those days with pride.

A NEW VILLAGE

I distinctly remember the Passion Play, which the Church Youth Group performed under the supervision of the church minister, Reverend Roy Neehall (deceased).

Albert Baldeo (deceased) played the part of Jesus, and he played it well. The Life and teachings of Jesus Christ greatly influenced my life. When I was a baby, my parents had baptized me as a Christian, but in my heart, I once again accepted Jesus as my Lord and Saviour.

My eldest sister, Myrtle, played the part of the Woman from Samaria. For one week, the group performed the play in the meadows, which formed part of the grounds of the church and the headmaster's home where we lived.

My entire family stood in our front gallery to view the dramatic presentation each day.

Albert Baldeo became a Presbyterian Church Minister in his later years.

The Government of Trinidad and Tobago granted my father a Scholarship for one year to study post-primary methods at the London University Institute of Education, and he left in the middle of that year. We missed him very much. When he returned home in the middle of the following year, he brought us lots of beautiful costume jewelry and English clothes.

He encouraged me to write the Bursary examinations for Naparima Girls' High School. I did so and won a bursary for that school. It was like a college exhibition since Naparima Girls' High School provided my books free, and I did not have to pay tuition fees.

I started High School in the next academic year, which commenced in January. My sister, who had started High School in the year before, was one class ahead of me. The school was big and the classrooms occupied more than an acre of land. It was located on La Pique Hill, which is part of the San Fernando Hill that overlooks San Fernando.

San Fernando is the second most populous city in Trinidad and Tobago, in the southwestern part of Trinidad. The boundary in the north is the Guaracara River. In the south lies the Oropouche River. To the east is the Sir Solomon Hochoy Highway, and in the west is the Gulf of Paria. San Fernando is known as the industrial capital, because of its proximity to the oil refinery in Pointe a Pierre.

The school principal seemed very strict, but my form mistress was a very nice teacher. Every day after school, my sister and I walked with other friends down to the San Fernando wharf to take the bus to travel home. San Fernando is hilly, and the walk was long and tiring.

In June of that same year, my eldest sister got married in a fabulous wedding ceremony at the Penal Presbyterian Church.

I was a bridesmaid. The bridal retinue walked across from the Headmaster's house to the church on a red carpet.

A grand reception followed at the Penal Presbyterian School Hall, which was also in close range. My eldest sister, who was crowned Bazaar Queen several times at the church and school bazaars, was a stunning bride. Her six sisters were bridesmaids. Everyone remarked that the chief bridesmaid, the sister I used to call "Billy," looked gorgeous in pink. All the other sisters looked pretty in blue net.

My father had bought six playful goats a few weeks before the wedding. I loved to play with them and feed them. They appeared very sensible and reminded me of the white lambs my father had bought in my earlier years.

In horror, I looked on as the cooks killed, skinned, and cooked them.

When they served the meat at the wedding reception, I could not eat it. I stopped eating goat meat from that day onwards.

That same month my eldest brother married a beautiful girl and they had two lovely daughters from that marriage. He was married before, divorced, and had two wonderful children with his first wife. Since I was young when he first got married, I do not recall much about his first wife. My older sisters found her amicable.

In October of that year, my father received another promotion to Inspector of Schools, North Eastern Counties in Trinidad. This necessitated a move to Sangre Grande, where his office and the Inspector's residence were located. He arranged for my eldest sister and her husband to occupy the Headmaster's house until the end of the school year. He did that so Florabelle and I could stay with them to finish the school term at Naparima Girls' High School while the rest of the family moved to Sangre Grande.

When my eldest sister and her husband had their first child, Flora and I went to stay with one of my brothers and his wife in Vistabella. We walked to school from Vistabella.

It was a long walk up and down steep roads, but we enjoyed it. Our cousin and her mother, who are now both deceased, lived next door, and we spent a lot of our spare time with them.

With the move to Sangre Grande, we had to find new schools in that area. Since my older sister had won a Government exhibition, she obtained a transfer to St. Augustine Girls' High School. As I had won a bursary specifically for Naparima Girls' High School, my father had to pay my tuition fees and buy my books for any other school.

Travelling expenses for both of us from Sangre Grande to St. Augustine added up to a tidy sum.

My father was the only breadwinner in the family.

My mother had to give up her needlework job with his promotion to the new position. He made plans to send me to a secondary school in the district of Sangre Grande. I relied on my father's judgment. He had already purchased my uniform and schoolbooks when he reconsidered and decided to make the sacrifice to send me to St. Augustine Girls' High School together with Florabelle.

I was happy with that decision for two reasons. I did not like the pair of manly looking shoes I was required to wear as part of the uniform for the school in Sangre Grande, and I wanted the company of my sister to attend school.

Sangre Grande was a modern and delightful village with many retail shops and a cinema. We lived in the brand new Government Quarters at Picton Street, where many other Government officials lived. The Guaico Presbyterian Church was not far away, and we went to church every Sunday.

On weekends, my sisters and I went for long walks and visited friends.

Two older sisters and one brother were teachers. One of my sisters taught at Fishing Pond Presbyterian School and another at the Plum Mitan Presbyterian School. My brother taught at Guaico Presbyterian School. Three of them left Trinidad after a short while to further their studies in the United Kingdom, and we missed them very much.

On school days, my sister and I walked out of Picton Street on the mornings, with our heavy school bags, to the main road and down to the Sangre Grande junction to catch the bus to Tunapuna. The bus made stops in Guaico, Valencia, passed through Waller Field, then to Arima, D'abadie, Tacarigua, Arouca, and then to Tunapuna. From there, we boarded the school bus together with dozens of students from neighbouring districts. The bus took us inside the school compound of St. Augustine Girls' High School.

On afternoons, the school bus picked up the students and dropped us off at St. John's Road in St. Augustine. From there, we took the Sangre Grande bus back to the main road in Sangre Grande, from where we walked all the way back home. It was difficult to walk such long distances with our heavy school bags, but we enjoyed chatting with each other while walking.

We joined the school choir and took part in school concerts.

We also played hockey, table tennis, and netball. My mother and father became members of the Parent-Teachers Association, and I felt very proud of them each time they came to the school to attend an event.

The school had a small lunchroom. It was not big enough to accommodate the many students who had lunch in the school. A group of my classmates ate lunch under a large tree on the school grounds. One day, one of the girls brought to school a single cigarette and matches in her lunch kit. She lit the cigarette and passed it around to each of us who were having lunch together, to take a puff. Not wanting to be a prude, I took a puff when it was my turn.

One of the senior girls passed and saw us and reported us to the School Principal.

She sent messages to us to report to her office. Both the School Principal and Assistant Principal reprimanded us for bad behavior.

They warned us they would expel us from school if ever there was a recurrence. I detest the scent of cigarette smoke and have never touched another cigarette since that day.

Two years after we moved to Sangre Grande, my father received another promotion as Senior Inspector of Schools for the South region, and the family had to move south once more.

My sister and I stayed in the school's dormitory in St. Augustine to finish our schooling. What I do recall about the dormitory was that it housed just twenty girls. The school chose girls who lived far away. Both my sister and I had valid reasons to stay there. San Fernando to St Augustine was a very long drive, and there were no highways in those days.

The dormitory was not very big. It was like a house, with a living cum dining area, a kitchen, and five bedrooms. There was an enclosed staircase at the front of the building and another at the back leading to a back door.

It was not air-conditioned, and it was modestly furnished. Windows were wide open during the day to let in fresh air. There was one bathroom for all twenty girls to use.

Each bedroom had two double-decker beds, two desks, and two reading lamps. Four girls shared one room. The girls never lacked for food or refreshment. We received three full meals – breakfast, lunch, and dinner. For snacks, we had tea, juices, and biscuits each day after school at around 3.00 o'clock in the afternoon.

The matron was very pleasant, and although she tried to be strict with the students, she had a soft heart and was willing to compromise or turn a blind eye. For instance, to save on electricity bills, the matron instructed us to turn off the lights by 9.00 p.m.

One night, we were studying for a Biology test, and the matron walked around in her noisy shoes, which made a click-clack sound, and shouted out, "Time to turn off all lights." We still had a lot of work to revise, but one of our roommates signaled to three of us to turn off the lights. We knew she had something planned. As we listened to the clicking of the matron's shoes retreat in the darkness, our roommate signaled to us to take the reading lamp under the beds. We huddled in two pairs under the beds, studying until we were sleepy and could study no more.

The next morning at breakfast, the matron said, "Last night after I told everyone to turn off the lights, I saw lights coming from under a door in one of the rooms. Anyone care to shed some light on that?" There was complete silence, and after a few moments, my roommate said, "I am sorry about that. I had to finish a project to hand in today."

The matron said, "You could have asked me for more time. I would not have refused. Talk to me next time," and she ended the matter there.

From that day onwards, we became closer to the matron and always consulted her when we needed to study later than the time for turning off the lights. She was most accommodating.

I recall another incident where one of the girls was hungry late at night. She sneaked into the kitchen to grab something to eat. The matron walked in on her but did not scold her. She helped her to get something to eat and told her to come to her next time instead of stealing.

At the time we stayed in the dormitory, the Curepe Presbyterian Church was under construction. The Christian Endeavour Society held meetings in the school auditorium on Wednesday nights and the Matron took us to those meetings.

They were very inspiring and we took part in several events. I started singing duets with another church member and received many compliments about my voice. I was a member of the school choir, and I would always remember Miss Lenore Mahase, the music teacher, who trained me to sing.

She played the piano beautifully, too. She conducted the choir with her hands and used her fingers to show us how to form the words as we sang.

On occasions, the matron allowed us to go to hockey matches when St Augustine Girls played against other schools in Port of Spain. One of the older girls in the higher form was in charge of us. I remember our school chanted this at the matches:

St Augustine High, St Augustine High

Yiketty Yackety aye, aye, aye!

Show 'em how to play girls, show 'em how to fight,

Yiketty Yackety aye, aye, aye.

I must say that we had more privileges in the dormitory than at home. Staying in the dormitory was a part of my school life that I will never forget.

An older student, who was also staying in the dormitory, lent me a book, *The Power of Positive Thinking,* written by *Norman Vincent Peale.*

It was the most interesting and educational book I had ever read.

The contents of that book helped to influence my life in a most positive way. I learned at a very early age that, *'I could do all things through Christ who strengtheneth me.'*

Sometimes it was difficult for my father to drive from San Fernando to St. Augustine to pick us up on Friday evenings. He told us that if he was unable to come for us, we should travel to Couva on the train and spend the weekend with my uncle. My uncle agreed to that arrangement.

Travelling on the train was fun. Many of our school friends travelled on the train, which journeyed from Watts Station in St. Augustine and made stops in Cunupia, Longdenville, Chaguanas, Carapichaima, and Couva.

One of our school friends lived at Couva, and when we spent weekends there, she would invite us over or go with us to the cinema.

We made friends with a Spanish family who lived near to our uncle. We often visited them and they taught us to dance the castians and meringue. These pastimes helped us to improve our mental abilities and prepared us for our studies.

My parents eventually built a brand new home at Roy Avenue in Marabella, and we took up residence there. We loved our new home.

The years flew by and soon it was time to write the Senior Cambridge Local Examinations.

Florabelle who was repeating the exams also wrote the exams together with me. The examination for Bible Knowledge was on 1st December, my sixteenth birthday. I prayed to God for a distinction on my birthday.

On the Sunday night before the English Language examination, our Spanish girlfriends held a party at their home in Couva, and my sister and I attended. We knew that we should have been at our uncle's home preparing for the examinations the next day, but could not resist the party.

When we received our results, we were thrilled. Both my sister and I obtained the Senior Cambridge School Certificate Grade Two with distinctions and credits in several subjects including English Language and Bible Knowledge. My parents were extremely proud of us.

A school friend celebrated her seventeenth birthday with a lovely birthday party at her home in Siparia.

She invited both my sister and me. My father was friends with her father, and he took us and waited for us until the party was over.

I recall hearing the beat of the latest hit song, 'Save the last dance for me', which they played at the party.

We attended our graduation ceremony for St. Augustine Girls' High School. Both my sister and I received prizes for the highest grade in English Language.

Our parents were present at the graduation ceremony, and they kept telling us how happy we made them. My father was strict and did not allow us to attend the graduation dance later in the night.

Up to that point in my life, I had tried to keep abreast of my older sister, Florabelle. I soon realized that I did not want to follow the career path she had chosen which was Teaching. Thereafter, we went separate ways. I was to follow a path entirely different from that of my brothers and sisters.

LOOKING FOR A JOB

After graduating from St. Augustine Girls' High School, I decided that I did not want to do Advanced Levels. I wanted to obtain a job and earn a salary to help my parents.

At age sixteen, I thought it would be best to help my father with the finances for the home. My older brothers and sisters were married or studying abroad and living in their own homes. Sybil and Addison were in England furthering their studies. Rosabelle was a teacher, and Florabelle who graduated from High School together with me got a teaching job at the Vistabella Presbyterian School. My two younger sisters, Jamella and Arabella were attending St. Joseph's Convent in San Fernando.

I sent out several applications to branches of Barclays Bank D.C.O. I always wanted to work in a bank since I thought banks opened to the public for half a day and I would work only until noon. The replies to my applications all stated that there were no vacancies. Nevertheless, I was not discouraged. I prayed to God for a positive response.

Well-meaning folks told me the banks in Trinidad only employed local and foreign whites, and more recently, Chinese and coloured persons. Many people said I had little chance of obtaining a job at the bank since I was of East Indian descent.

My father told me that one of my sister's friends worked at the Harris Promenade branch of the bank in San Fernando, where he maintained his accounts, and it was possible I could be as fortunate as she had been.

One day in April, I received a letter from the Couva branch requesting that I call for an interview with the Manager. In dismay, I noticed that the date for the interview had already passed.

The letter had arrived two days late. I ran to tell my father. He was at home that day.

I showed him the letter signed by the Manager and told him it was of no use. My father got up from his chair and told me, "Get dressed now. We will go to see the manager, and I will do the talking."

I panicked, as I had nothing to wear. My older sisters were at work. I needed to borrow an outfit. I opened my elder sister's wardrobe. She had many pretty clothes. I grabbed a skirt and a blouse and threw them on. It did not take my father long to get dressed. He was pacing the floor in the living room. I ran a comb through my hair and rushed out of the bedroom. I did not want to keep my father waiting.

My mother was in the kitchen and was unaware of what was taking place. My father called out to her to let her know where he was taking me. She wished me good luck as we sped off in my father's car.

Upon arrival at the bank, my father went to the secretary, who introduced herself. She was an attractive coloured person.

He told her he wanted to see the Manager about an important matter. He asked her for the Manager's name, and she told him it was Mr. Wright. She was very pleasant and polite, and in less than a minute, she ushered us into his office.

Mr. Wright shook hands with us and asked what he could do for us. My father took out the letter and explained that it was delayed in the mail. Mr. Wright was an Englishman and seemed kind and understanding. He told us of experiences he also had with the mail, and he and my father carried on a casual conversation.

Mr. Wright stated that he was very impressed with my school results and job application. I recall answering one question. "Where do you place in the family?" to which I replied. "Eighth." The interview was over before I knew it. He then advised that I would have to write the bank's entrance test before he could consider me for the job, and he set a date for me to do so in the following week.

My father took me to write the test at the appointed time. He waited at the home of my uncle in Couva until I was finished writing it. The Accountant at the bank advised me that I would hear from them when he corrected the papers.

During that time, while my father was waiting for me at my uncle's home, my uncle's neighbours visited them. Those visitors told my father that their daughter worked as a clerk at the Couva bank for six months, and the manager did not confirm her in the position after her probationary period. They told him he should not allow me to accept the job, as the same thing would happen to me.

They also told him of their friend's daughter, whom the manager dismissed after the six-month probationary period. My father told them that the decision was mine to make and he would not allow the experiences of others to affect my choice of a job. Besides, he was confident that I would do well and be confirmed after the six-month probationary period.

He related this to me when he picked me up after the test. I thanked God for such a wise father.

.

I GOT THE JOB

On 1st. May, I was sitting on the front porch of my parents' home at Marabella. I saw the Manager driving towards my home. He stopped at the house and called me. I ran downstairs to meet him. He told me I was successful in the test, and I was required to report to work on Monday, the 3rd. May at the Couva branch of the bank.

I was surprised that he came in person to ask me to start work. My parents were pleased that I got the job. I thanked God for answering my prayers,

On the first day of the job at the bank, the Manager's secretary introduced me to all the members of staff. It was a sub-branch and a few staff members were working there.

The Accountant, Mr. Wilbert Smith, was very nice and understanding. There were two other female staff members and a male who was a cashier. The total number of staff was seven including the Manager.

The Accountant told one of the female staff members to teach me the daily routine at the counter. She explained everything, and I understood. She said I was a quick learner. We did everything manually. Savings Ledgers were large brown books, which hurt my back each time I took them down to enter transactions for customers.

This seemed like one hundred times a day. We posted entries in customers' passbooks with a pen. If we made an error, the Accountant had to initial it. This deterred me from making errors.

Many of the customers were illiterate and worked on the sugar cane estate in the area. In those days Trinidad grew sugarcane and manufactured sugar at the sugar-cane factory for export. The British overseers also maintained accounts at the bank.

We had to take thumbprints of the illiterate ones on the withdrawal slips.

What I liked about those days was that we had the opportunity to handle every transaction for the customer, such as savings withdrawal, deposits, foreign bank drafts, bills of exchange, mail transfers, and fixed deposits.

I learned a lot about banking from doing those transactions.

Although the bank closed at noon, we had internal work to do, which caused us to work late. It was not a half-day job as I had thought it would be, but I enjoyed it.

After attending to each customer, we passed the vouchers through a cubbyhole to the cashier, who handled the cash part of the transaction. Every day, a manual waste sheet and a daily balancing summary had to be prepared to balance the day's input.

The waste sheet was a trial balance of the day's work. A staff member prepared this manually from the day's vouchers. First, the staff member sorted the vouchers to correspond with the books of the general ledger and listed them on the sheet with a pen.

We used the only available adding machine to get the totals. Clerks responsible for the various functions agreed their figures against the waste sheet. The cashier balanced his cashbook against the total cash received listed on the waste sheet. The clerks responsible for savings and current accounts listed the vouchers and balanced the figures against those on the waste sheet.

If one person's figures were short by one cent, everyone had to stay back, sometimes until late at night, to find the error. I found balancing to be a challenge. I loved helping my coworkers look for the errors and did not mind working late, although my parents worried each time I worked late.

The bank opened half-days on Saturdays too, but many times, we worked all day on a Saturday if one of the staff members could not balance his/her ledger.

The current account ledger was a large pack of ledger cards on which the ledger clerk entered customers' daily transactions using a mechanized business machine. This was part of the afternoon duties for one of my co-workers. After she used the machine, it was my job to enter the same information on the customers' statements using the same machine.

The machine gave totals of the debits and credits, and we compared these against the waste sheet. Sometimes the figures did not balance, and we spent hours finding the errors. Sometimes it was the fault of the waste clerk, who entered current account figures under savings or vice versa.

Every three months we worked savings interest manually. It was a tedious exercise but I enjoyed it. When my six-month probationary period was up, the manager called me into his office and told me he was pleased with my progress on the job. He advised that he was confirming my position as a bank clerk. He handed me a letter of confirmation.

The first person I told was Florabelle. I confided in her a lot. We were close as she was closer to my age, attended the same schools, and had similar experiences and friends as I had. That week I worked late, so I sent her a note to let her know of my confirmation. I also quoted from the hymn, which we both loved, *'To God be the glory, great things he had done.'* We sang that hymn for our first communion at the Marabella Presbyterian Church where Reverend Francis Muttoo influenced my life by his inspiring sermons.

All the new communicants, among who was Cyril Paul (deceased) who became a Minister of the Presbyterian Church, loved that hymn. That afternoon when my sister gave my parents the good news, they were overjoyed. My father thanked God that he did not allow my uncle's neighbours to discourage me from taking the job.

Soon after my confirmation on the job, the manager returned to his homeland in the United Kingdom. Another manager took over management of the sub-branch. He was very serious and had a habit of pacing the floor and keeping an eye on the staff.

We later learned that it was not his intention to look over our shoulders. He served in the military for a while and was a war hero. He did not communicate much with the staff and I do not remember anything of significance during his tenure at the bank in Couva.

I was sad when Wilbert Smith, the Accountant married one of the female staff members and left to work in Jamaica. I received my best training in the budding years of my career under his skillful guidance. He had persuaded me and other staff members to study for the Institute of Bankers Examinations and even tutored us after work, to make sure we succeeded.

Because of his encouragement, I studied and gained a Certificate in Banking from The Chartered Institute of Bankers, London, with subjects including Elements of Banking, Law, Economics, and Bookkeeping.

When my brother returned from England as a qualified attorney, I was scared to ask for time off to attend his engagement party. It was the end of the bank's financial year, and everyone had to work late balancing the books.

I told Mr. Smith about the engagement at around 9.00 p.m. that night. He called my mother, who was waiting at my uncle's home in Couva, to collect me. He told her if he had been told him about it much earlier, he would have allowed me to leave work. I will never forget his dedication to his job and his kindness towards me.

One of the female staff, Merlyn, and I became close friends.

I spent a weekend at her home to attend a party in Siparia. I also attended her wedding.

SUSIE'S ACCIDENT

My sisters and I attended the Children's Carnival show at Naparima Bowl in San Fernando in the month of February. The sponsor of the show selected sixteen girls from the audience. He chose me and asked me to join the others on the stage. They wanted to choose a *Queen for a day*. The girl who got the most applause from the audience would be the winner.

I was reluctant to take part, but my sisters insisted that I go on stage. The sponsor told us to parade in front of the audience and judges. I thought, *Why not*? It seemed like fun. I walked around the stage casually and waved at the audience. The loud cheers I heard each time I waved amazed me.

The judges eliminated the unpopular girls, and I and another girl ended up on the stage. The chief judge announced that I got the most applause.

He was about to make the final announcement that I was the *Queen for a day,* and the other girl was the runner-up. The other girl's boyfriend jumped on stage and threatened the judges, telling them that if his girlfriend was not selected as the *Queen,* he would instigate violence. No one wanted that to happen. The judges called me aside and discussed it with me. To avoid any unpleasantness, I agreed to be the runner-up and the other girl to be crowned Queen. To me, peace is more important than a crown for one day. I received a pair of earrings as my prize, and I gave them to my eldest sister, Myrtle.

That year, my father was granted long leave. He went to England for a six-month vacation to visit my two sisters who were both studying there. Sybil had since married and taken up residence in London. Rose had gone to London earlier in that year to further her studies. My mother and two younger sisters, Jamella and Susie, were to join my father after three months. Neither Florabelle nor I could join them, as we had to work. The plan was for us to stay with my two older brothers.

During the early part of the first three months that my father was abroad, Susie, who had fallen out of the window when she was two and a half years old, had written the Common Entrance Examination for secondary schools and passed for the secondary school of her first choice. She asked my mother's permission to visit one of her friends who lived across the highway. The friend had promised to meet her with her older sister so they could cross the road safely. My mother agreed.

Later in the day, I was sitting on the porch, and I saw a car drive up to our home. A man came out and lifted someone from the vehicle. The person had bandages all over her body. When I looked closer, I saw that he was holding Susie in his arms.

I ran inside to call my mother. By that time, the man had walked up the stairs with Susie.

He explained that while she was crossing the road to return home, he accidentally knocked her down. He took her to the hospital and waited until the doctors attended to her. She told him where she lived, and he brought her home.

My mother broke down in tears when she saw her. She thanked the man for his honesty. We were all grateful that he had taken my sister to the hospital, waited until the doctors attended to her, and brought her home. Nowadays, people are not that honest. If it were someone else, my sister may have been a victim of a hit-and-run accident.

With that new turn of events, and my sister bedridden, my mother was unsure if they would have been able to join my father in England in a few weeks.

We prayed for her healing so they could join my father in London.

She got better in time to make the trip. My sister, two brothers, and I stayed behind, as we had to work. Our niece, Shalimar, stayed with us.

We loved her very much and missed her when she returned to her mother's home.

We had fun during the three months that my parents were in England. Addison fried chicken for my sister and me one evening. He was very proud of his accomplishment and invited us to partake of the dish. Although we appreciated his kind gesture in helping us to prepare dinner, we almost died with laughter. He burnt the fried chicken black. We forced ourselves to eat it to please him.

Both our brothers were protective of their sisters. On Saturday, I went downstairs in the open area and I saw a man peeping at me from the bushes. I screamed and ran upstairs shouting, "A man is in the bushes." My eldest brother, Gilbert, heard me and ran downstairs with a stick to protect me.

Addison and his friends arrived home at the same time, and they checked around the whole area to make sure that the man was not still lurking in the bushes. We saw him running away. It was a scary experience.

When my parents and sisters returned home after their vacation in London, there was another wedding in the family.

Addison landed a job in St. Lucia as the Registrar General. After a few months, he returned to marry his fiancée in a memorable wedding at the Marabella Presbyterian Church. All my sisters and I were bridesmaids at that wedding. We were happy to have Bebett join our family. She was a qualified pharmacist. Newspaper headlines for their wedding read, *Registrar General in St. Lucia weds Pharmacist from Penal in Trinidad*.

At that wedding, we wore green chiffon dresses. It was rather breezy that day. As we stood outside of the church waiting for the procession to begin, Jamella, my younger sister, and I chuckled as our stockings blew in the breeze. At the reception at the bride's home, we met many of our friends and we had a wonderful time.

The happy couple left to live in St. Lucia, but returned to Trinidad when my brother was appointed Assistant Legal Adviser at Texaco, Trinidad.

HELLO WORLD

After Mr. Smith left the Couva branch, we did not have a permanent replacement. It took a while, but eventually, someone replaced him.

A new, vibrant Manager also took over the branch, and he was well-liked in the community. Under his astute management, the branch's business grew. He gained a large number of new accounts and assisted in the development of Couva.

The Bank's Head Office upgraded the sub-branch to a full branch and that was a great achievement. He employed more staff members to accommodate the increased business. I learned a great deal from that manager and dreamt of being like him one day.

A new staff member, Jennifer Hamid, joined the bank at that time and we became close friends.

I continued to enjoy my job and became quite efficient at my duties. I also found time to assist others.

Whenever a savings ledger could not balance at the end of the month, the Manager pointed to me and told the Accountant, 'give it to the expert to find the error.' I always found the errors, and the Manager always commended me.

I was required to perform duties as a cashier at the time the Government decided to replace the large British Caribbean notes and coins with Trinidad & Tobago currency. This entailed a great deal of sorting at the end of the day, but I never experienced problems in balancing both currencies.

My evening duties were to help the manager compile statistics for the advances control sheets. Advances meant loans and overdrafts. The manager checked the calculations daily, and he always commended me for my accuracy and efficiency.

My father wanted me to leave the bank to go abroad to further my studies. I wrote several letters to universities abroad and received several positive responses. The replies came to the bank's address at Couva.

In those days, the Manager received all branch mail. He noticed the return addresses of the universities on the envelopes addressed to me. He called me into his office one day and told me that I should stay in the bank as he felt that I had the potential to go very far. I was happy to hear that because I always had a secret ambition to be a bank manager. I knew that was what my father wished for me, and I wanted to please my father.

My sister and I had often discussed going abroad to study together. She married another teacher and decided to stay in Trinidad. I was her chief bridesmaid at the wedding. After her wedding, I decided that I would make banking my career since I did not want to go abroad alone.

I told my father my decision, and he said that I should do what I thought was best.

Bank Managers changed again, and the branch continued to grow. More businesses came on stream, and business owners opened accounts at the bank. The Manager employed additional staff, and I made many new friends.

At my sister's wedding, I remembered the old saying, *Three times a bridesmaid, never a bride*. I was a bridesmaid at three weddings. When would I be a bride?

After six years in the bank, I wondered if I had made the right decision to stay in Banking. I felt I was not getting anywhere. I enjoyed the job, but the bank's method of doing staff reports was very secretive. Each year, we signed blank staff reports. The manager filled in the details afterward. We had no way of knowing where we stood, nor were we advised if our performance was up to standard by the new Manager.

I observed that only men got promotional opportunities. Although the Accountant rotated our jobs, there was no grading system. We did not know if we were moving upwards or downwards.

At least I had my long leave to look forward to the following year. I was entitled to four months from June. After seven years of service with Barclays Bank D.C.O., an employee could have expected a break with full pay and a travel grant. I needed that vacation.

I told my father about my forthcoming leave and he suggested that I visit Rose and her family in Germany. He said that since the bank would stand the cost of the trip, I should make use of the opportunity.

Another person. Eddy Walcott, was acting for the substantive Manager who was on vacation. He was a very agreeable individual and I felt at ease conversing with him. I told him that I was making plans to go to Germany to spend part of my vacation. My sister's husband was in the Royal Air Force in Wildenrath, Germany. My other sister, who lived in England, had since returned to Trinidad with her husband and their two sons.

The Acting Manager told me he knew a girl at another branch who was also going on long leave and who needed a companion to travel.

I told him I would love to meet her. He arranged for me to meet her to discuss plans. Sylvia Lee Seyon had relatives in New York and Toronto, and friends in the United Kingdom so we added those places to our itinerary. I convinced my father to allow me to go to those other places. He suggested that we invite her to our home to have lunch, as he and my mother wanted to get to know her.

Sylvia was a very amiable young woman who had travelled before and my father liked her right away.

He felt at ease that I would be in capable company and that she would be my travelling companion. When we sat down to have the meal, my father said a prayer for our safety during our trip.

I will never forget that year in early June when my father drove me to the airport. My mother and sisters accompanied us. Sylvia was at the airport with her relatives. It was a tearful occasion for my family because I was the eighth child, and it was my first trip abroad.

I caught a glimpse of a person at the airport who had joined the bank in recent times. We were both becoming interested in each other. I knew he went to the airport to see me off, but he kept a distance away as he did not want to upset my father. My father never allowed his daughters to go on dates, and he did not know about my friend. We were lucky that we met each other at our workplace. Before I met him, other guys were interested in me, but since I could not go out with them, things never moved forward.

I waved to him and he waved back. That wave meant a lot to both of us. We understood each other.

My eldest sister met her husband when my father went to London on a Government scholarship. Two of my other sisters met their husbands in London when they went there to further their studies. Another sister who was a teacher met her husband, who was also a teacher at the same school in which she worked.

When Sylvia and I entered the plane, I said to myself, *"Hello world. Here I come."* It was my first trip on a plane and I was very relaxed. The air hostesses served us with lots to eat and drink. It was very different in those days compared to nowadays, where they no longer serve food on some flights.

When we landed in New York at John F. Kennedy Airport, my friend's cousin and her husband were there to greet us. I was meeting them for the first time, and they were friendly. They drove us to their home in Jamaica in Queens New York.

Jamaica was a middle-class neighbourhood where many immigrants live. They had a nice home there and they gave me a separate room from Sylvia's.

Notwithstanding, I admit I was homesick. I missed my parents, brothers, and sisters.

The following day, Sylvia's cousin took us into the city on the bus, and we went shopping. There were many bargains available. Clothes were much cheaper than in Trinidad. I did not want to spend much money in New York, though, as that was just our first stop in the itinerary. I bought one dress for my youngest sister, Arabella [Susie], and a few souvenirs.

When we were returning home on the bus, we had to stand, as there were no vacant seats.

A woman came behind me and touched me on my shoulders. When I turned around and she saw my face, she said she was sorry. She said that from my back, she mistook me for her friend who had become a movie star. I was flattered.

The next day the whole family went to see a fantastic musical show at the Radio City Music Hall on Broadway, and afterwards, we had dinner at a fancy restaurant. The show was fantastic and the dinner sumptuous.

Every day, Sylvia's cousin took us to see a new interesting place, and I was enjoying our stay in New York. One day, she took us to Chinatown in downtown Manhattan. It rained that day. It was crowded too. Many people were shopping. I never liked crowded places and I felt sick. After buying fish, she took us back to her home. When we returned home I became sicker, and after eating dinner, I went to bed.

The next day we boarded a flight to Toronto. I was feverish and cold and wore a sweater but that did not help me to feel better. When we landed in Toronto, it was cold and windy and I felt worse.

Sylvia's brother took us to his apartment. He said the apartment was small and could only accommodate two people. He planned to stay next door with his friend. I thought it was very nice and considerate of him.

He promised to call a doctor to visit me as he saw how ill I was. He told me to lie down and rest and to cover up with a blanket. I did that and fell asleep.

When I woke up, I coughed a lot and had a swollen nose. The doctor came just as I awoke, and Sylvia brought him in the bedroom to see me. She was worried about my illness. The doctor gave me an injection and tablets and told me to rest. He said I needed to stay in bed for one week as I had a bad case of the flu. My heart sank. We were staying for one week in Toronto and I had to be confined to bed. Sylvia was disappointed and so was I. We had planned to have much fun, as her brother was also a fun loving person. What a damper!

The following day I received a letter from my father. There was no electronic mail in those days. He wanted to know if I was enjoying myself. I could not hide the truth from him and I replied to him, telling him I was ill with the flu and confined to bed.

His reply was quick, as I received a letter from him before the end of that week. He said if I wanted to return home, I should change my flight arrangements and go back home. I knew I could not do that and leave Sylvia alone, so I replied to him and told him I was going ahead with our plans. It was an opportunity of a lifetime, and I wanted to go through with it.

In spite of the doctor's orders to stay in bed, I joined Sylvia and her brother for drives around the city in his car. We took photos at Couching Park and Yorkville and walked on Yonge Street. I could not appreciate the beauty of the city, as I was feeling too weak and ill. I did not even care to look at the shops and did not buy a souvenir there.

I was still ill when we flew to London. It was a long flight, but I slept on the plane. We arrived there early in the morning, and we took a cab to the Royal Overseas League, where we spent the week.

The Royal Overseas League is a non-profit Commonwealth private members' organization, and both Sylvia and I became members of that League before our trip. It was a beautiful hotel with luxury accommodation overlooking Green Park in London.

We had booked a lovely, spacious room for two with a Roman bathroom. The warm weather in London was like home in Trinidad. I felt better right away but still went to see a doctor. He gave me a new medication and within two days, I was as good as new.

Sylvia was happy that I was well again. We explored all the popular sites in London. Two other friends joined us. We took photos on the Bridge of the River Thames and had fun at Battersea Park. We visited the beautiful Kew Gardens, shopped on Oxford Street, and rode in the double-decker buses. The mini dress and wedged heel shoes were the latest crazes in London, and my friend and I stocked up our wardrobes with lovely mini dresses and wedged heel shoes to take back to Trinidad.

I was having a good time and was glad I did not cut the trip short to return home.

Soon the day came for our trip to Germany. We took the bus to the airport, and that was a big mistake. There was a massive pile-up of traffic along the way and the bus took double the normal time to get to the airport. We missed our flight to Germany. When we arrived at the airline counter, the clerk told us that the flight had just taken off and that they would accommodate us on the next available one, which was leaving in two hours.

We had no choice but to wait, so we sat down at one of the airport restaurants and had something to eat until it was time to board. Meanwhile, my brother-in-law was waiting at the Dusseldorf airport in Germany for us. He had checked and found out we missed the first flight and would be on the next one. Soon, it was boarding time.

The boarding clerk announced that passengers should board the plane.

We were excited. The biggest part of our adventures was about to begin. The flight was not long, and it was pleasant.

When we landed at the Düsseldorf airport our brother-in-law was there waiting for us. We apologized to him for having him wait long, but he said he understood. He told us my sister was at home. She was looking forward to our arrival. I had not seen Rose in six years since she left to live in London and moved to Germany. I too could not wait to see her.

As my brother-in-law was in the Royal Air Force, they lived in the camp in Wildenrath in a beautiful two storey - house. The weather was lovely and it was like home in Trinidad. My sister and her two young children, Paul and Sharon, whom I had never met before, were at the door to meet us.

Rose greeted us and hugged us. We did not notice anything different about her, except that she looked lovely in a mini dress.

The children were very nice and talkative. I met them for the first time. We sat down, chatted, and had something to eat. As the house was in an air force base, there were intermittent noises from low-flying planes. The windows shook every time a plane flew over the house.

My sister showed us our room and we unpacked our stuff and went back downstairs.

When we returned downstairs, we saw my sister with a suitcase standing at the door. She said, "Okay guys. I am going to the hospital." Both my friend and I looked at her in amazement. "What is wrong with you?" I asked.

She pointed to her tummy, which seemed normal. She said, "I am having a baby. It is due." We laughed because we both thought she was joking.

I said, "But your tummy is barely noticeable."

She said, "It is time. I'd better hurry."

My brother-in-law smiled and said, "Bye. Take care of the children. I will be right back." Our jaws dropped. It seemed unbelievable.

When my brother-in-law returned from the hospital, he said my sister would not be delivering the baby until later that night, so he took us all for a drive to see Wildenrath.

All the houses in the camp were similar to the one my sister and family lived in. There was a long building where the single officers lived. We saw a clubhouse, a large airstrip, a shopping centre, and the hospital. Further down the street, there were cafes and a large forested area. There was not much to see in Wildenrath and my brother-in-law promised to take us to Monchengladbach in Germany, which was close to Wildenrath. He also said that Wildenrath was close to the border, and he would take us to Holland. That sounded very exciting to Sylvia and me.

The next day, my brother-in-law woke us up. He told us that my sister had a baby boy and would come home later in the evening. God had blessed them with two boys and one girl.

Sylvia and I helped prepare the meals that day and then we walked around the back of the house.

There was an apple tree in the backyard, and we picked apples and enjoyed them. We took a walk in the neighbourhood.

It was quiet and there was no one in sight. In the evening, my brother-in-law took us to the hospital to bring home his wife and their handsome newborn son, Mark.

The Royal Air Force was putting on an air show at the airstrip the following day. My sister could not go with the young baby, so she stayed at home with the children and told us to go to the show with her husband. He drove us there but had to park the car far away from the airstrip.

We had to walk across in our mini dresses and wedged heel shoes to where the crowds were standing and sitting. As we were walking, we heard lots of hoots and whistles. My brother-in-law said the officers were trying to get our attention.

When we reached the crowd lots of his friends came around and asked for introductions.

The air show began and we saw the most amazing air tactics displayed by airplanes. "The Red Arrows" somersaulted dozens of times and air force military jumped out in colourful parachutes before our eyes. It was the most breath-taking event I ever experienced.

One night Cyrus took us to the clubhouse, which was crowded with Air Force officers. Once again, we heard loud whistles and hoots and Cyrus said the officers were trying to get our attention. Many of the officers, who did not meet us before, crowded around for introductions. My brother-in-law, who was a Sergeant in the RAF, was firm with them and kept them at a distance.

I inserted a coin in a slot machine and hundreds of Deutsche marks came tumbling out. Everyone watched in amazement. My brother-in-law collected them and ordered drinks for everyone.

It was the practice of the residents of the camp to have parties in their basements. Every night, a different couple held a basement party. We attended quite a few of those parties, and they were delightful with good music and lots to eat and drink.

One night a couple invited us to a basement party at their home. They told us it was a 'cave-man' style party. We thought it had something to do with the food. When we got there, we saw everyone dressed in 'cave-man' outfits.

We must have looked ridiculous to them as Sylvia and I were dressed in mini dresses and high heels. Despite that, we had a merry time at the party.

My sister's home in Wildenrath was closer to the border in Holland than it was to other parts of Germany.

Cyrus took us across the border to discotheques in Amsterdam and sometimes to other parts of Germany. It was my first time going to discos, and in

Holland and Germany at that. Cyrus' two friends from the RAF always joined us on these jaunts. They followed us in their car.

The discotheques had strobe lights that flashed on and off in time to the music. A large iridescent ball hung in the middle of the dance floor and created a swinging atmosphere. We had fun dancing to disco music. Cyrus' brown eyes seemed to flash in time to the music when he was on the dance floor. The men always ordered cognac and cola, which seemed to be the "in thing." I settled for the cola with no cognac.

Once on our way back home from a discotheque in Holland, Cyrus stopped the car at a lovely park, turned on the car radio, got out of the car, and danced in the green meadows. He was a fun-loving person.

Holland is a spectacular place. The scenery is beyond description. The architecture of the buildings, the brightly coloured tulips, windmills, green meadows, and the clean streets all captured my attention. Germany is also a clean and beautiful country. I have many treasured memories of my visits to those places. In later years, I visited Germany again, and details of all my travels are in my book Travel Memoirs with Pictures: Exploring the World.

Sylvia and I had planned to make the return voyage home by the ss Antilles, which was a popular ship in those days. However, she received bad news from her family, who wanted her to return home earlier than planned. I agreed to her change in arrangements to travel to Trinidad by air since it would have taken almost two weeks to travel home by ship. We had a small problem getting a flight from Germany to London to coincide with the date for our flight from London to Trinidad.

Cyrus's boss arranged for us to fly to London in a Royal Air Force Jet, which was going to London on the day we wanted to leave Germany.

Travelling on that Air Force Jet was an awesome experience and one I would never forget.

With sad hearts, we left my sister, her husband, and the children, but we left with beautiful memories of a wonderful holiday in Germany.

When we returned to Trinidad, my parents, brothers, and sisters gathered around me to listen to my fantastic adventures. I had much to tell them.

Although Sylvia and I had wondered about the reaction of our relatives and friends when we landed in Trinidad with mini dresses and wedged - heel shoes, we started a fashion trend. All the girls in the bank cut and hemmed their skirts and dresses to make them short.

My younger sisters loved my dresses, and I shared a few with them. My parents never commented that my dresses were too short. I still have many dreams of that trip.

The Bank changed its policies a few years later and removed long leave from its benefits, so staff members who joined later were no longer entitled to that benefit.

A WEDDING PROPOSAL

After such an exciting vacation, I returned refreshed to work at the Couva branch and met several staff changes. Another senior staff member joined us to supervise the foreign trade aspect of the branch as the branch's business was growing. The branch had a new Accountant, and he was a very hard worker.

When I saw his enthusiasm, I once again felt motivated to make banking my career. The Annual Management Accounting Planning document was a new requirement introduced by the bank. The purpose of the document was to set targets and, at the end of the financial year, to compare them against the actual figures achieved. Variances would reflect the true performance of the branch.

Having worked at the bank's Head Office before his transfer to Couva branch, the new Accountant was familiar with it.

The Branch Manager relied on the new Accountant's ability to complete the document for which there was a deadline. The Accountant had no assistant, and he asked me to help him with the document. It appeared to be very complicated and entailed a great deal of work with figures and calculations. I grasped that opportunity to learn all about it, and I managed to complete it under his expert guidance. He praised me for my aptitude for learning and taught me many of his other duties.

Eventually, the Bank introduced mechanization for all accounts. Staff had to transfer all the information for Savings accounts from the large brown books to ledger cards, like that of the current accounts. We had to work until late into the night for many nights to complete that exercise.

One of my co-workers, Rashiff, celebrated his birthday with a birthday party at the home of his parents before I went on my trip abroad. He had asked me to stick the cake with him, and I did. He was also at the airport to see me off when I was leaving on my vacation. We corresponded with each other while I was on vacation abroad. When I returned to Trinidad, our relationship grew stronger.

We had lunches together, but never went on a date. I did not discuss our relationship with my father.

One day at home, I went into my father's library to get a pen. His diary was open on his desk. The open page did not escape my glance. He had written, *Pray for Brenda to get a husband.*

I flicked the pages backward, and I saw that he had written that same line above his other posts as far back as three months. It occurred to me that my father wanted me to get married.

The next day at work, I told Rashiff about the diary notes.

He promised to go to see my father to ask him for my hand in marriage. In those days, the guy had to write a letter to the girl's father to ask for her hand in marriage and he did that.

When he turned up at my home with the letter, I was like a fish out of water. *What if my father turned him away?* I hoped and prayed that my father would be polite to him.

Before he came, I told my sister why he was coming to see our father. I hid in my room when he turned up at our home. My sister let him into the house and called my father. My father was polite to him. It was the first time they met each other. After a long chat, he told him he would discuss the matter with me and get back to him. My father did not know I was eavesdropping in the next room.

When Rashiff left, my father called me and told me about the conversation and he showed me the letter. He asked if I wanted to marry Rashiff and I said 'yes'.

He told me we had his blessings and to make plans for an engagement party.

When I told Rashiff about my father's response, he was elated, and so was I. My father must have felt God answered his prayers. There was no longer a need to write about it in his diary.

In July of that year, Rashiff and I became engaged in a small ceremony with close friends and relatives at my parents' home. We had both selected the diamond engagement ring at a popular jewelry store the week before the engagement party. I proudly wore it.

The Bank's authorities transferred me to the High Street, San Fernando Branch, because of bank policy. The reason was that we were two staff members who were engaged and had plans to marry the following year. Husband and wife could not work at the same branch.

High Street Branch in San Fernando was much closer to my home. It was a big branch and different to Couva branch. It was in the heart of San Fernando and on the street with all the retail businesses.

There were separate departments for Savings, Current Accounts, Clearings, Foreign Trade, Credit, and Securities.

The lady Accountant discussed my new job with me on my first day. She did not introduce me to the Manager, who was an Englishman.

One of my fellow workers told me that the Manager never spoke to junior staff members. I would only see him when my annual staff report was due and I had to sign it in his presence.

In those days, Englishmen managed most of the branches of the Bank. The Head Office of Barclays Bank D.C.O. in the United Kingdom made all managerial appointments.

Barclays Bank owned the majority shareholding of the Bank in Trinidad.

The Accountant advised that she was putting me in charge of the Clearings Department.

I had to collect all cheques from the waste clerk, whose duty it was to collect all vouchers from the cashier. I had to list them on forms for branches or banks on which the cheques were drawn. I had to send the lists for collection to the respective banks or branches. There were no computers in those days, and I had to use an adding machine with a pull-handle. I had to balance the totals with the figures on the waste sheets, which another clerk prepared on a huge machine.

In spite of the large volume of cheques, I balanced the figures daily. 'First–shot' was the term used. That was the easy part. The most difficult part was getting the finished product signed by two signatories.

The signatories were supervisors of other departments, and although I placed the completed clearings on their desks by 2.00 p.m. each day, they signed them when they finished the work in their departments. Most times this was long after 4.00 o'clock.

Many evenings, I had to stay back late to insert them in their respective envelopes.

The Accountant soon recognized my ability to get the job done in an efficient manner. She transferred me to the Credit and Securities Department as a Securities clerk. This was new to me. My supervisor was clear in her instructions and easy to understand. I admired the patience she exercised with customers, the way she dressed, and her graceful manner. I enjoyed working with her very much. There was one other staff member in the department, and she was an experienced security clerk. She taught me everything about securities, and we got along well.

My supervisor also dealt with loan customers. She requested my help to interview customers and complete Statement of Affairs forms. I considered that as a learning opportunity and grabbed it.

When my supervisor resigned from her job to go abroad to live, another amicable person replaced her. Although she was firm, she was knowledgeable and very jovial. It was a pleasure to work with her.

WEDDING BELLS

My fiancé, Rashiff, and I made plans for our wedding in August of 1970. A few weeks before the wedding, The Black Power Movement surged and staged an uprising in Trinidad. Rashiff and I were worried about whether we would have to postpone the wedding.

The leader of the movement stated that its purpose was to protest to the Government of the day that black people could not get jobs at the foreign-owned local banks. Those were scary and uncertain times, and we prayed for a peaceful resolution.

The Government soon curbed that situation. It was God's will that Rashiff and I exchange vows, and that is what we did in a simple but splendid wedding ceremony at the Marabella Presbyterian Church.

My youngest sister, Arabella [Susie] was my chief bridesmaid, and two of my nieces were bridesmaids.

As I walked up the exquisitely decorated aisle on my father's arm, I saw Rashiff standing at the altar with his cousin, who was the best man.

Rashiff was smiling, and his gaze was on me in my lovely, flowing bridal gown and exquisite bridal bouquet. He looked very handsome in his dark suit. I knew I was doing the right thing. He was the man with whom I wanted to spend the rest of my life.

The ceremony started on time, and before we knew it, we had taken our vows and the Church Minister pronounced us man and wife. Signing the register was the next step.

My eldest sister, Myrtle, sang my favourite song at the church at my request, 'Each step I take, I know my Saviour leads me.'

There was a reception at the home of my husband's parents at which all of our family and friends were present. My mother was not well and could not host a reception.

She was a semi-invalid and could not attend the wedding.

Our wedding cake was a stunning replica of the bank in which we worked and met. The food was East Indian and very sumptuous.

We spent a wonderful honeymoon in Barbados at the Blue Waters Beach hotel. Upon our return, my father gave me a plot of land at Couva as a wedding present. Since we could not afford to build our home right away, we lived with my husband's parents for two years. Two of my husband's sisters and brother were young and unmarried. Only his eldest sister was married and living in her own home.

Rashiff's parents treated me as a daughter, and I experienced no problems while I lived there.

Because of my marriage, I requested a transfer to the Chaguanas branch, which was nearer to my new abode. Chaguanas was a bustling town with many retail businesses. My husband continued working at the Couva branch of the bank.

I believed our marriage was blessed because from then onwards, both of our careers blossomed.

I took up duties at the Chaguanas branch when my husband and I returned from our honeymoon in Barbados. My training and experience at the Couva and High Street branches placed me in a favourable light with my superiors. I was a 'Girl Friday,' assisting everyone. No job was too difficult for me.

The Accountant was always very busy, and it was the time of the year to prepare the Annual Management Planning Accounting document.

I told the Assistant Accountant that I learned to do the documents at the Couva branch and that I could help with it.

He told the Accountant and they were happy to pass it to me to prepare.

The Assistant Accountant told me that since he had never done the plan before, I should teach him to do it. I did so. He appreciated my willingness to share my knowledge. We met the deadline for submission, and this pleased the Manager and the Accountant.

In October that year, the bank changed its name from Barclays Bank, Dominion, Colonial, and Overseas, to Barclays Bank International Ltd. This was the first step towards the localization of the bank, a subject that had been under much discussion with the prevailing Government of Trinidad and Tobago and the Head Office of Barclays Bank in the United Kingdom.

I continued to do my best at work. In April of the following year, the Manager recommended me for promotion to a Supervisor. The Bank's Head Office accepted his recommendation. That was my first step up the corporate ladder. I enjoyed the job very much and found it rather challenging. The staff for whom I was responsible were supportive, and that made my job easy.

That year I took my vacation together with my husband, and we spent one week in Tobago. When I returned to work I learned that the Bank was about to computerize its operations.

The Bank informed staff members that they needed staff at the Computer Center. Anyone interested in working at the Centre had to take an aptitude test. I was enthusiastic about the new step the bank was taking. I applied to take the aptitude test and I did so with many other staff members from branches throughout the island.

A few days later, the Manager of the Computer Centre called me for an interview. He told me I had placed among the top three persons on the island. That was a great achievement. He wanted me to work at the Centre, which he planned to open on 20th, July. He said that workers would have to work shift hours. I declined the offer because

I had found out earlier that I was pregnant with my first child.

As I was pregnant, my husband and I wanted our own home. My brother, former Registrar General at St. Lucia, returned to Trinidad to live. He was working as the Assistant Legal Adviser at Texaco and was moving to a house on the Texaco camp at Pointe a Pierre.

He offered to rent us his home at Vistabella. I told my branch Manager I wanted a transfer to any branch in San Fernando since my husband and I planned to live there. He was very disappointed that I had to leave the Chaguanas branch, but he granted me my wish.

I recommended a long-standing staff member to take over my job as Supervisor of Accounts and Foreign Trade. That staff member worked at the Harris Promenade branch in San Fernando at the time I was applying for a job at the bank.

I mentioned her in chapter three in this book. After her marriage, she requested a transfer to the Chaguanas branch.

The following year, the bank localized its operations. The name of the bank changed to Barclays Bank of Trinidad and Tobago Ltd. This meant Barclays Bank International Limited sold its assets to the local bank.

I received the transfer I requested in that same month. I reported to the Pointe a Pierre branch. That branch handled all the financial transactions for workers at the oil refinery.

The Accountant told me that he wanted me to take over the job of Supervisor of Accounts and Standing Orders. In those days, that was a manual operation. When I saw the piles of debit and credit vouchers lying scattered on the substantive Supervisor's desk, I wondered if I could do that job. It was frightening.

I prayed to God for wisdom to handle that job. The Supervisor from whom I was taking over the job told me she was glad to be going to a Port of Spain branch since she could no longer cope with that position.

I got down to work and in less than a month, I had everything under control. I had spare time to help the cashiers make up pay packets for the workers in the oil company every week.

Making up pay packets was another tedious job and one which required the help of everyone including the Manager, Accountant, and Supervisors. In those days, customers preferred to take home their weekly wages in cash to avoid going to the bank to take out money. There were no Automatic Banking Machines.

In spite of everything, my desk was always clear, The Supervisor of Foreign Trade and Treasury felt I had less to do than she had. She kept complaining to the Accountant that she had too much work to do and that he should switch her job with mine.

In August, one of my friends from the Couva branch of the bank passed away in Canada after a critical illness, which required surgery. Her death saddened me. I was almost seven months pregnant, and after her funeral, I kept dreaming about her. In a dream, I was walking through the cemetery, and she kept calling me. I did not answer her and ran away.

BIRTH OF MY CHILDREN

My husband and I were blessed with the birth of my son, Adrian, in the month of October. I experienced serious complications but survived to be the proud mother of a beautiful baby boy. I could not help but look at him in amazement, as he lay in his glass cot next to me. He was so perfect in every way. I counted all his toes and fingers several times. I loved him with all my heart.

The greatest miracle in my life was to give birth to a perfect little being. I felt an instant bond between us, and I thanked God for blessing my husband and me with a lovely son.

I was due to return to work at the end of my maternity leave. Getting a responsible helper to look after my son was a problem.

Many mornings I had to take him to my eldest sister, Myrtle, who had moved to live at Marabella, downstairs of my parents' home. She offered to take care of him when the helper did not come to work. My father spent lots of time with my son. He loved him very much. Many times, he would steal him away from my sister and take him to the grocery to pamper him with goodies.

My mother's illness had worsened, yet she enjoyed making snacks for him. Because of their caring ways and the help of my loving sister and parents, I was never late for work.

When I returned to work, the Supervisor of Foreign Trade and Treasury again asked the Accountant to switch her job with mine, and he agreed. She was always complaining about having too much to do. He asked me if I would mind doing so. Although I was hesitant to change jobs so soon, I agreed, as I considered it an opportunity to learn more about banking.

In less than a month, I handled that job with ease, and still had spare time to assist with pay packets in the usual way. That Supervisor still did not find time to help anyone and continued to complain about having too much to do.

In August of the following year, my husband and I took our paid vacation together. We wanted to visit my sister, Rose, and family, who had moved from Germany to Cirencester in England. My younger sister, Jam, went with us, but we did not take our son since he was less than a year old. My eldest sister, Myrtle, who was always there to help me out, agreed to look after him for the two weeks we planned to be abroad.

We had a fantastic time in England. We visited Stratford-upon-Avon and many other beautiful places, but we missed our son very much. I bought him many presents and looked forward to being with him again.

When we returned home, he was calling Myrtle, '*Mommy*' and clinging to her. He looked at both Rashiff and me as if we were strangers. Our coaxing did not encourage him to go home with us. He refused our attention and stayed with my sister. That hurt us a lot, but I did not give up.

I spent the next day at my sister's, convincing him I was his mother. I took a suitcase filled with all the stuff I bought for him to entice him. It was hard work, but I won my son back again.

Upon my return to work, I learned that the Manager of the Pointe a Pierre branch had returned to the United Kingdom. Another Manager with whom I worked at the Couva Branch took over his position. I had grown accustomed to his management style in Couva, and working with him once again was no problem.

The Accountant fell ill, and the Manager asked me to act as the Accountant. I was pregnant with my second child. I acted as an Accountant for three months before proceeding on maternity leave. Despite my pregnancy and frequent feelings of nausea throughout the full term, I reported to work every day and performed my duties.

Many times, I had to leave my desk to go to the ladies' room to vomit, but I always returned as if nothing was wrong.

When the acting period was over, the Manager advised me he had recommended me for a promotion to a Senior Supervisor upon completion of my maternity leave. He was pleased with my consistent high level of performance.

I gave birth to our daughter, Michelle, on 6th November. She was the most beautiful little girl in my eyes. I thanked God for giving my husband and me a daughter to complete our family.

When our son, who was just two years old, came to the nursing home to see us with his father, he asked him, "Daddy, who is that?" My husband replied, "She is your sister," to which our son said, "Oh." He accepted her right away as his little sister.

A NEW EVOLUTION

After my maternity leave ended, I returned to work. The branch manager told me he was transferring me to the High Street, San Fernando Branch to await my promotion to Senior Supervisor. He said the Bank had also transferred him to the High St. Branch as the Assistant Manager. What a coincidence!

The transfer to the High Street branch was the launching pad of my career. The branch was quite familiar to me, as I had previously worked in the Clearings and Securities Departments. The female Accountant was replaced by a male, and he put me in charge of the Treasury and as his Assistant. I also had to oversee the audit department. The duties were not new to me as I had experience in those areas in other branches in which I worked.

The Computer Centre was still computerizing the bank's records.

Staff did not have time to look after their homes and children in the proper manner, as we had to spend the greater part of the twenty-four-hour day at the office preparing documents for the Computer Center. We worked late every day and into the night.

Sometimes we worked until the early hours of the morning without any compensation, transferring files and passing amendments to computerize thousands of accounts.

Fortunately, I had an older sister, Myrtle, with a golden heart who looked after my children when the helper left for the day.

One brave woman with legal qualifications, and who worked at another branch, held meetings with staff from the branches island-wide, and encouraged the majority of the staff to form a Staff Association.

The purpose of the Association was to meet with Management to discuss salaries, uniforms, and other conditions of service. The Bank's Management turned down the Association's proposals, and members proposed a one-day sickout to get them to change their minds.

My husband and I were in a quandary. Should we take part in the sick-out? Both of us worked in the organization, and there was a possibility we could both lose our jobs. We were also looking to buy our own home.

At one time, we had applied to the Bank where we worked for a loan of TT$15,000.00 to buy 15000 square feet of land, in a residential area where one of my sisters lived. The Bank's Head Office, which was in Barbados, declined the loan. The letter we received stated, *we were biting off more than we could chew*. That tells you how small our salaries were if we could not have serviced a $15,000.00 loan over five years with the joint incomes of my husband and myself.

We had sold the plot of land at Couva that my father gave us as a wedding present to buy land in a new development in Gulf View, which was close to us. The land developers could not get approvals to complete the developments, and neither could we get the approvals to build a house there.

We thought long and hard and prayed about the sick-out and whether to take part in it. I remembered these words in the Bible. "*Trust in the Lord with all thy heart. In all thy ways acknowledge him, and he shall direct thy paths.*" I remembered another quote in the book of Ecclesiastes, "*A Time to be quiet and a time to speak up.*"

We made up our minds and stayed home on the day of the sickout. Our children were young. My son was three years old and my daughter was seven months old. I had worked in that organization for fourteen years and my husband had eight years of experience on the job. It was a chance we had to take.

The day we stayed at home, fear crept into our minds. We were fearful of losing our jobs.

I dismissed that fear and told my husband I saw a house at the top of the street where we lived with a "For Sale" sign. I wanted to have a look at it. He agreed. We took both children and walked up the road to the house.

The owners welcomed us and showed us the inside of the house. We liked it. Without hesitation, we told the owner we were ready to buy the house and we would call him to arrange a down payment. It was settled. We returned home and realized that we had committed ourselves to buy the house without knowing if we still had jobs. Worse yet, we had insufficient money in the bank to buy groceries that month.

That night we were looking at the news on Television. The Bank's Managing Director made a plea on

Television stating that all staff members were welcome to return to work the following day. He said that the Bank had accepted the Staff Association as the bargaining body for staff. He confirmed that the jobs of all staff were secure and they were considering the Association's proposals for better salaries and conditions.

They were also prepared to pay retroactive payments to all staff.

My husband and I thanked God. This meant we could purchase the house we saw. We returned to work, applied for it, and our employers granted a housing loan to us with no problems. We bought the house in June of that year and kept the Gulf View property to give as a legacy to one of the children.

The Registration and Certification Board recognized the new Association, and its first Collective Agreement took effect from June in that year. The Association amended its name and constitution and became the Bank's Employees Union.

Unionization transformed relationships between management and employees and this professional approach brought with it many staff benefits.

After the Bank completed computerizing the Savings and Current account ledgers, branch staff no longer had to deal with tiresome and time-consuming bookkeeping, ledger posting, manual listings, and balancing. Staff no longer had to calculate Interest and other charges manually. The Computer Centre computed and generated these charges.

Customers benefited from this technology since they could go into any branch to handle their transactions. There was no longer the need for late work except on rare occasions, and we no longer had to lift heavy ledgers to enter customer transactions. It was a wonderful transformation for staff and customers, and the start of a new evolution in banking.

DEATH OF MY FATHER

That year, my father passed away after a heart attack. It was the first time I had experienced the death of a loved one. I felt as if the world had ended. I walked around in a daze. I was married for five years and had two young children. Yet I missed him and kept recalling the good times we had shared.

On the day he became ill and was admitted to the nursing home, he seemed to know he was about to die. He called all his children around him and spoke to each one. I do not know what he said to my siblings, but he asked me to bring my two children to see him.

I returned to my home, which was not far from the nursing home, and brought back my two children. He placed his hand on the head of both of them and prayed for them and blessed them.

He told us he loved us and he was sure that God would continue to bless our lives.

We all stayed at the nursing home with him during those last moments. He asked for something to eat. One of my sisters asked the nurses for soup and fed it to him. He then lay down on the bed and took his last breath. It was one of my most painful experiences to witness the death of my beloved father.

That evening, we discovered in his desk drawer, full details of how he wanted his funeral conducted. He had selected and purchased a family burial plot. He also left a letter addressed to his wife and children.

In the letter, he quoted from the book of Proverbs Chapter 31: 10-30. Details of that letter are in his memoirs. The name of the book is *"Memoirs of Dr. Andrew Moonir Khan: Journey of an Educator.* I compiled that book from his diaries and notes and revised it in 2014.

My father knew he was about to die and was well prepared.

In June, we moved into our new home, and in July, I obtained my driver's license. Later that month, our family went abroad on vacation to Buffalo and Toronto.

In Buffalo, we stayed at my youngest sister, Arabella, fondly called Susie. She had married and migrated with her husband to the United States. After graduating from St. Joseph's Convent, San Fernando, she completed a degree in Languages at the University of the West Indies, Jamaica. She met and married a very nice Guyanese national. They both pursued their studies and gained Doctorates at the University of New York at Buffalo. My sister had come a long way, after falling out of the window at one of my parents' former homes and getting knocked down by a car in her youth. We were all very proud of her.

In Toronto, we stayed at my friend, Jenny, who had worked at the Couva branch of the bank. She had married and migrated to Canada.

When we left on our vacation, we did not take our baby daughter with us as she was just a few months old. We left her with Rose and her family who had since returned from London to live in Trinidad. We took our three-year-old son.

We had a lovely vacation but I missed my baby daughter. Buffalo was a very nice city and the shopping was great. Toronto seemed much brighter than my earlier trip with Sylvia when I was ill. We visited the zoo and many tourist attractions. Of course, we went to the fabulous Niagara Falls and had lots of fun but I kept thinking of my daughter.

When we returned home, my daughter reached out and clung to me. She seemed to be telling me that she missed me. She did not forget me the way my son did when I went to England. I vowed to always take my children with me on all vacations.

When we returned to work my husband received a promotion as a Supervisor at the Coffee Street branch in San Fernando.

We were lucky to be both working in San Fernando and close to our home. We praised and thanked God for all his blessings.

At the High Street branch, I had a three-month stint as Supervisor of the Loans department and another three-month stint as Supervisor of the Securities Department. My experience as a securities clerk helped me to succeed in both those positions.

The bank ceased work on Saturdays. It was a big improvement in our lives. The staff members were gratified as they had longer weekends.

The Manager told me that he was pleased with all areas of my performance. He put me in charge of the Foreign Trade Department as the Senior Supervisor. This was another stepping-stone in my career. I had excellent staff to work with and we gave our customers superior service. When the bank inspectors came to do an audit of the department, they gave us a clean Inspection report.

The manager was again pleased. He told me I made the Foreign Trade Department seem easy to handle. He was therefore certain that I could manage the Credit Department. The Credit Department is responsible for loans and overdrafts to customers and is one of the top departments of the bank.

The opportunity came in April of that year when the Manager's Assistant of Credit moved to another position. The Manager told him to hand over the Credit job to Brenda Mohammed. When I went to take over the job from Michael Ali, he got up from his seat, pointed to it, and said, *"You are in the hot seat now."* He then moved to another desk. He did not teach me the job, so I had to learn through trial and error.

Fortunately, I had experience in granting loans and handling securities and it was not a big problem for me to learn details of the credit department. The job entailed assisting the Manager and Assistant Manager with loans and overdrafts to customers and supervising the large departmental staff, of which there were two junior supervisors in charge of Republic Loans and Securities.

I learned a lot from the manager, who was very meticulous. An error could not slip past him. As happened to all my favourite bosses, he was transferred to another branch and another manager assumed the position.

The new manager was easy to get along with, and it was business as usual for me. He had an excellent command of the English language, and I enjoyed reading his correspondence.

I considered myself very fortunate to have worked with all those managers as I learned something new from each one. I knew I was being groomed for higher responsibility.

My husband and I were enjoying working close to home. He dropped me to work on mornings and the children to school. It was convenient for our family. His branch manager suddenly informed him that the Bank's Head Office transferred him to the Mayaro branch of the bank. Mayaro is a very long distance from San Fernando.

Besides it being far away, the roads were also bad. We agreed that he should stay in his sister's beach house during the week and come home on weekends.

I had a live-in helper, so it was not a problem. However, although I had my driver's license, I never drove. How would I get to work, and how would the children go to school? With his transfer, we had to make urgent changes in our lives.

I applied for and obtained a loan to buy a car. That was my first car, and it was a yellow Toyota Corolla. Next, I took a refresher course in driving before venturing on the road. Two co-workers took me to work until I gained confidence to drive. My sister-in-law came on afternoons to take me for driving practices. Soon I was driving to work, dropping off, and picking up the children to and from school. I even offered other persons lifts in my car.

My husband and I were fortunate to get our vacation leave together at the end of the year.

The bank gave us vacation grants and we used them to go to Orlando for a grand vacation with our son and daughter, who were seven and five.

My younger sister, Jam, and a niece, Carrie, also accompanied us. We stayed at the Red Carpet International Hotel in Orlando, and every day we took the bus to the Transportation and Ticket Centre. From there, we boarded the Monorail to the Magic Kingdom. The children had a superb time, and they took many pictures with Mickey Mouse and Bugs Bunny.

We visited all of the major attractions such as Walt Disney World Village, Frontierland, Liberty Square, Fantasyland, and Adventure land. It was fun riding on a Carousel, and sailing through pirate strongholds and treasure rooms. Next, we took a 'danger-filled' cruise down tropical rivers of the world, tested our sharp-shooting skills at 'wilderness' targets, visited a haunted mansion, and saw a dramatic presentation of America's history, as all the American Presidents 'came to life' on stage.

We visited many other places of interest. Among them were Sea World, the world's largest, most elaborate Marine Park encompassing 135 acres. Show features were Shamu, a three-ton whale, a one-ton elephant seal, dolphins and other seals performing incredible feats in two air-conditioned stadiums.

Other attractions included Japanese and Hawaiian villages, a light and water show, pearl diving, a 'see and touch' tide pool and a 150,000-gallon aquarium. We also saw a ski show featuring Sea World's professional skiers in a raft of exciting feats.

At Circus World, ten minutes west of Disney World, Ringling Brothers, Barnum, and Bailey Entertainment Centre featured a live circus extravaganza with fifty performers including polar bears, elephants, clowns, aerialists, jugglers, and dancers. The trapeze performances were fabulous.

It was like meeting each of Hollywood's famous personalities in person at the Stars Hall of Fame. The World's largest Wax Museum featured two hundred stars of movies, television, and music in one hundred elaborate sets, recreating memorable moments from their careers. We saw a unique display of stars' signatures, hand, and footprints in the Plaza of the Stars. We could not go to Orlando and not visit Cypress Gardens, another tourist attraction. There we feasted our eyes on the splendour of the stately pines and spreading oak trees, toured caves and boulevards and took lots of pictures which still fill the album.

When we left Orlando, we went to Miami where we spent a few days in a hotel to go shopping. On the day we were about to return home the loud ringing of the fire alarm woke us at four o'clock in the morning.

We heard other hotel guests shouting, "Fire! Fire!' We jumped off our beds.

In a panic, I grabbed all of our passports and tickets and left everything else in the room. We ran out of the room and followed other guests down the fire escape. When we reached the bottom of the stairs, we saw everyone staring at us. They said it was a false alarm, but they still kept staring at us.

I realized that I was in a long, sheer nightgown with all the passports and tickets in my hand.

Rashiff was in his shorts and my sister and the children were in their nightclothes too. My daughter, Michelle, who was just five years old, was hiding behind me, and she said she saw everyone staring at us through my nightgown. We rushed back to our rooms in embarrassment, and although it was rather early, we got dressed and went to the airport to await our flight home.

It was a marvellous vacation. When we returned home, it was difficult to erase the wonderful memories.

The following year my eldest sister and I went to Puerto Rico for another exciting vacation.

We stayed at the Excelsior Hotel and did a lot of sightseeing and shopping.

FIRST APPOINTMENT

The bank was exploring ways to improve salaries and benefits for staff. Hired consultants and the Bank Employees Union conducted a joint job evaluation exercise to grade all clerical jobs.

All staff received retroactive payments as they graded jobs at a higher level than what we were being paid. Both my husband and I received a tidy sum each, which we put aside to help with the purchase of new appliances on our next trip abroad.

The country's economy grew with more oil and gas discoveries and foreign investments.

The bank benefited from the spin-off and expanded into thirty-four branches throughout Trinidad and Tobago.

It changed its name to Republic Bank Limited with a new logo and corporate signature.

The Manager of the High Street branch assigned me to the Penal sub-branch to provide relief for the substantive sub-manager who was availing of leave. It was a very new experience being in charge of a branch. I prayed to God for guidance, and I performed my duties well. In June of that year, when the sub-manager moved to Point Fortin Branch, the manager recommended me as Sub-Manager of the Penal branch. This was another step for me up the ladder of success.

The Personnel Manager from the Bank's Head Office went to the High Street branch to inform me of my appointment.

He told me both he and the High Street Branch Manager monitored my performance and my achievements in the short space of time I provided relief for the Penal sub-manager. They believed that the Penal sub-branch had a lot of potential for growth and that I had the ability to gain new business and develop the branch into a full branch.

I promised them I would do my best. I thanked God for my promotion, and I prayed for the wisdom to achieve the results my superiors expected of me.

In May of that year, the Bank hosted its first long service awards function at the Trinidad Hilton Hotel in Port of Spain. All the staff members with fifteen, twenty-five, and thirty-five years of service received awards. I received a silver wristwatch for fifteen years of dedicated service.

I took over management of the Penal sub-branch with a clear goal, which I set for myself, and that was to achieve full branch status within a year. The Manager's Assistant, Administration, and my Assistant in Credit and Securities gave me sterling support.

As I was new to the area, I relied on the staff to inform me of new developments in the area.

Norman Girwar, one of the clerical assistants at the branch, referred several prospects to me and drove me in my car to visit them to offer banking facilities. On every occasion, we gained new business and brought in several new accounts for the bank.

I granted many loans and overdrafts to deserving entrepreneurs to expand their businesses. For each new business, I sent a report to our Head Office.

The Managing Director's Assistant, Corporate Operations, and Development and the Managing Director sent me letters of commendation.

Every time I faced a difficult situation on the job, I prayed to God for the wisdom of King Solomon to deal with it.

One day I heard an irate customer quarreling loudly with a male staff member and asking to see the Manager. He was cursing, using obscene language, and carrying on because his employers did not send his salary to the bank. I heard the staff member trying to explain to him that it was not the fault of the bank and that he should check with his employer, but to no avail.

The staff member was scared and asked me if I would speak to him. I must admit that I was scared too, but I agreed. After all, I was the manager and it was my responsibility to ensure that customers were satisfied.

When the customer entered my office, he seemed shocked to see me. He covered his mouth with his hands, then apologized profusely for the disturbance he caused. He repeated a few times, "Miss, I am so sorry. If I knew such a young girl was the manager, I would have behaved myself. Please accept my apology. I will do anything you say."

After offering him a seat, I chatted with him and explained that sometimes there were delays in receipt of salaries from Government agencies.

He said he was a teacher and he once worked with one of the best headmasters at the Penal Presbyterian School. He was unaware that he was speaking of my father.

When I told him that Dr. Khan was my father, he was even more apologetic. He was happy with our conversation and left the bank in a good mood.

By June the following year, the staff of the sub-branch had exceeded all the targets set for business growth and was ready for upgrading to full branch status. It was amazing to see the changes in the village.

New large commercial buildings replaced most of the old buildings and the once slow-moving village looked like a bustling town.

I felt a sense of pride in the sub-branch's achievements under my management.

The Manager of High Street branch under whose overall control the sub-branch fell, congratulated my staff and me on this accomplishment. He recommended the upgrading of the sub-branch to full branch status and that I be promoted to its Manager.

Up to the time I proceeded on vacation in July, there was no response from Head Office on the Branch Manager's recommendations for the upgrading of the sub-branch to full branch status.

My husband, children, and I spent another most memorable vacation with my youngest sister and her husband who had since moved residence from Buffalo to Los Angeles, California. That was the sister who fell out the window, and was in a car accident when she was very young. She was brilliant and graduated with a doctorate in Spanish.

Her husband also had a doctorate in Spanish.

They were both College professors in colleges in California. Their son was almost two years old and was highly intelligent. He was their only child and talked a lot.

As my sister and her husband were busy with their jobs, my husband purchased Gray Line tour tickets for us to visit Universal Studios, Catalina Island, Farmer's Market, Hollywood Boulevard and other interesting places.

At Universal Studios, Gray Line gave us special treatment. We met our tour guide at the Hilton Hotel downtown Los Angeles, and from there they transported us to Universal Studios for a tour.

We travelled aboard a Glamor Tram, and a studio tour guide took us for a behind-the-scenes look at the world's largest movie and Television Studio.

Included in the tour were attractions such as the *Special Effects Stage*, the deadly shark attack by '*Jaws*', *a burning house, a flash flood, the parting of the Red Sea, a Train accident and collapsing bridge*, all of which seemed so real.

We saw a live viewing of the *Battle of Galactica* and sets and props from '*Land of the Giants*,' and '*The Six Million Dollar Man*'. We also took in live shows in the Universal Amphitheatre, including a Stunt show by actors dressed up as Cowboys. Our tour included a visit to *Castle Dracula*. We took our pictures with *'Frankenstein'*. We viewed the mansions of movie and television stars in fabulous Beverly Hills.

Afterward, the Gray line bus drove to Santa Monica on the shores of the Pacific and then to Farmer's Market for a treat with an international flavour.

Our adventure in Catalina Island began aboard a 700-passenger cruise ship designed for the Catalina service. We had intended to stroll the spacious decks and relax and enjoy the two-hour ocean voyage to that Magic Isle. Our daughter became seasick and vomited. While my husband was attending to her, he also became ill and vomited.

Then it was our son's turn to vomit. I was a very strong person who never suffered from travel sickness.

The sight and smell of vomit made me upset, and I became just as ill.

By the time we landed on Catalina Island, we were too weak to have as much fun as we had planned. Upon arrival at the beautiful Bay of Avalon, we did not go on any sightseeing tours, which involved boat trips. Instead, we explored the beautiful scenic island on foot.

We walked along the harbour and the beaches and visited all the souvenir shops. The Casino building caught our eye and we went on a guided tour of the twelve-storey building which was not occupied but was a tourist attraction.

The Avalon Theater, with its colourful heroic-size murals, acoustics that rank among the best in any public building anywhere, and its huge pipe organ that had many special sound effects was impressive.

We walked up the ramp to the mezzanine floor where the tour guide told us in words and pictures about the distinctive and fascinating features of the unique pleasure palace.

There were pictures of all the big bands that played in the Casino. The far-famed Ballroom was in a setting of soft lights and sweet music. The Casino tour concluded with a stroll around the balcony that encircled the building and a tram ride back to the town.

Late in the afternoon, the ship took us back to Los Angeles, a trip which we dreaded after the morning's experience.

We did a bit of shopping in Los Angeles and visited many other interesting sights such as the Hollywood

Bowl, Chinatown, the Chinese Theater and the world renowned Sunset Strip. To see the glitter of nightlights, transform the city into a sparkling wonderland is a sight no one should miss.

While in Los Angeles, I dreamt that I received a transfer to another branch.

Upon my return to work in early August, I received a call from the Managing Director's Assistant who requested that I visit him at the Head Office. I knew that my dream would come true.

When I went to see him, I was sure he would tell me about a transfer to another branch. I had no writing paper or notepad with me.

He congratulated me on my accomplishments at the Penal sub-branch and confirmed its upgrading, but said he would withhold that for a later date.

He explained that he required my expertise in another area. The Bank was seeking to set up the first Corporate Division to deal with large commercial accounts. They wanted the first such division in the South. He had already decided on the staffing for the division.

He had already told the Senior Corporate Manager and the Corporate Manager of their new appointments. They were proceeding on vacation and would not be available to give me any help until the date scheduled to open the division in September.

My new job was Senior Credit Analyst, of the Division.

He wanted me to do all the groundwork to make sure that the division could throw open its doors on September 6th.. He advised me of the names of the other staff members and said none of them could leave their current duties until the opening of the division. It was my full responsibility to ensure that the Division was ready for opening on the scheduled date.

Without handing me a sheet of paper to take notes, he opened a large file and related further details of how he expected the division to operate. I was stunned that he was giving me such an awesome assignment to complete in such a limited time. This was early August, and he wanted the Division set up and running on 6th September.

While I was astounded that he placed such confidence in me, I questioned myself. *Can I do this*?

He asked if I had questions. I was in a daze and could think of none. This situation was such a new one and he caught me unawares.

He shook my hands, wished me the best of luck, and told me to hand over the sub-branch to the new Manager before starting the project.

As I drove back to South after that meeting, I realized that my dream had come true. Thoughts crowded my mind. *How was I going to handle this assignment on my own?*

Was this a test? Should I have told the M.D.'s Assistant I could not do it in that short time? Suppose I failed?

Worse yet, I had taken no notes and had to rely on my memory. I once again prayed to God for his aid. I was not the kind of person who gave up easily. My motto was and still is, *Never give up. Reach for the sky.*

When I returned to the branch, I advised the staff of my transfer and new assignment. They were sorry that I had to go. The sub-branch had accomplished a great deal under my management and they felt it was too soon for me to leave.

The new Manager reported to the branch as scheduled and I handed over to her.

The Manager's Assistant, Administration organized a lovely farewell party for me. They gave me an unusual tall ceramic vase for my home as a parting gift. I appreciated the kind gesture but I was sad to leave.

CORPORATE DIVISION

When I went home, I worked out a plan as to how to proceed with my new assignment. I reported to the High Street Branch the next day to plan and execute my strategies. It was another challenge in my career, and I was going to accomplish that feat. I was not going to fail.

I needed to identify the accounts and request the files of the corporate customers from every branch in the South. That meant meeting with all South Managers at their branches to go through the files. I met with them, exchanged discussions, did the paperwork, and obtained the files.

I designed the systems and procedures for dealing with the customers and their accounts, and prepared a Handbook.

With the permission of the manager, I worked in the kitchen of the Pointe a Pierre branch because I had no office.

I also had to supervise the construction of the building. The building, which was to house the new Corporate Division in Pointe a Pierre, was still under construction late in August.

The Premises Manager in Head Office ordered the furniture from an office furniture store in Port of Spain. To my surprise, the owner of the office furniture store was my friend, Sylvia, who had travelled with me to New York, Canada, London, and Germany. She had left the bank after the trip and opened her own business. We had lost contact with each other because of our busy schedules. Sylvia had exquisite taste, and she ensured that the furniture matched the decor.

On the day that the Corporate Manager took up his assignment at the

Division, the furniture arrived and Sylvia came to help to arrange them.

When I showed the Corporate Manager the work I did on the systems and procedures, he complimented me on a job well done. When the Senior Corporate Manager turned up for work, he commented that the Division looked as if it always existed.

He too complimented me on the Handbook I prepared and the customer files I selected from the branches.

The next day, when the other staff members reported for duty I again received kudos. The secretaries had desks and materials to work with, and the other analysts found their workspace well laid out. They were happy to work in an office where everything was in place. The biggest test was when we threw open the doors to the customers and everything worked smoothly.

The Managing Director's Assistant came to visit the Corporate Division one month after we opened to the public.

He was impressed and told me I did an excellent job and he would bear that in mind.

In October, my dear mother passed away. All the family missed the Saturday evenings we spent at her home. We all gathered at her home every Saturday without fail. She never wanted us to leave without having dinner. Her helper prepared the meal. Many bank staff attended her funeral. I had lost both of my parents. I threw my energies into my work to rid myself of a deep sense of loss.

As we had a small staff in the Division, we became a close-knit unit. On special occasions, we each took a dish and had a hearty lunch together. We invited the bank's attorneys to join us sometimes since we had a close association with them. They handled mortgages, debentures, releases, and other legal matters for the bank's clients. We had fun while we worked and I recall those days with pleasure.

The Corporate Division South was a great success and the Bank wanted to open a North office. The Managing Director's Assistant sent a staff member, who worked in one of the north branches, to learn from me the various procedures for establishing the North Division. She got the job of Senior Credit Analyst when the North Division opened.

The Senior Corporate Manager took early retirement from the Bank. We organized a large cocktail party with staff and customers for his farewell. We were very sorry to see him leave. Another senior Manager took over the job. He was knowledgeable and very thorough, and it was an edifying experience working with him.

After a few months, I gained a promotion as a Relief Manager upon the prior recommendation of the Managers at the Corporate Division. My duties were to provide relief for managers proceeding on vacation. The staff of the division held a small farewell party for me at Soong's Great Wall restaurant in San Fernando. Lobsters and champagne were on the menu. I also received a three-tiered gold necklace as a farewell gift.

BOARD APPOINTMENT

In July 1984, the Bank sent eighteen staff members on a one-week Managerial Effectiveness Training Course run by the Institute of Management and Labour relations at the Mount Irvine Hotel in Tobago.

Both my husband and me were selected to attend. We received training in Leadership and Management skills. My group of six participants received awards for an effective presentation in the role-playing exercise. It was the Bank's intention that all participants would receive managerial appointments in due course.

In November 1985, the Bank installed the first Automatic Teller Machine at the Park Street branch.

The 'Blue Machine' as it was called was a great success with customers.

The same facility was added to other branches and convenient places in Trinidad and Tobago.

I sold my Toyota Corolla motorcar and bought a brand new Nissan Bluebird. It did not have power steering. With my appointment as Relief Manager, I gained the opportunity to work in several branches all over the island and meet many new customers and staff.

I was enjoying this very much, but driving long distances in a vehicle without power steering created back problems for me, and I experienced severe pains from my neck down, and my lower back and legs.

I visited my doctor and he told me I had an extra rib in the neck area and needed an operation to remove it. He also said I had a curved spine, which resulted in scoliosis. I felt I could not handle an operation, and I prayed to God not to have to go through that trauma.

The Ministry of Foreign Affairs seconded my younger sister, Jam, to work in the Trinidad and Tobago Embassy in New York. They gave her a beautiful apartment in Waterside Plaza, Manhattan. When I had my vacation that year, I visited her together with my eldest sister, Myrtle, to spend a few weeks.

My husband could not get leave, so he could not join us. During that time, I tried to forget about what the doctor had told me.

After the holiday, I had to go back to driving all over the island to provide relief for other managers, and I felt the pains more often. I longed for a change of duties.

In January 1986, the Managing Director of the Bank requested that I call to see him at the Head office. I took along my son with me since he wanted me to drop him off to Long Circular Mall. I was working at the branch in that mall. He waited downstairs while I took the elevator to the fourth floor to meet the

Managing Director who greeted me upon my arrival.

He offered me a seat, and then he smiled and told me that the Board of Directors had approved my appointment as the Manager of the Penal branch, effective 17th. February 1986. He congratulated me and gave me a package containing details of my emoluments.

As a Manager, I was entitled to an increase in salary, a new motor car every three years, a computer, a cell phone, an entertainment allowance, and other benefits. I thanked him for his confidence in my ability, and after a brief chat with him, rushed downstairs to give my son the good news. He was the first to learn of my promotion, and he hugged and congratulated me.

Upon my arrival home that evening, I told my husband and my daughter. We held a thanksgiving function the following week. When I started work at the Penal branch, the pain in my neck went away and never returned.

My career was moving in the right direction, and my health had improved. God answered my prayers, and I did not have to do neck surgery.

The drive to Penal was short, compared to the driving while I was a Relief Manager. The Bank bought me a brand new Nissan Laurel motor car equipped with power steering and comfortable seats for my back and neck.

As I had worked at Penal when it was a sub-branch, I had no problems getting used to the area again. In fact, all the customers remembered me and welcomed my return. The staff members were very pleasant and hardworking.

After my appointment at the Penal branch of the bank, I had to attend a one-week resident course in Management at the Trinidad Hilton Hotel. Managers from various companies attended. I was the only woman on that course. I also had the benefit of participating in a Credit Appraisals Techniques Course run by The Institute of Bankers, London.

The course was held at the Bank's Head Office, and all of the Bank's managers attended.

Topics covered were Financial Management, The Traditional Approach to Credit, Management Accounting-Based Lending, Project Appraisal and Financing, and Corporate Business Development. These courses prepared me for my role as Bank Manager.

That same year, my elder brother took early retirement from his job. He left his job as Assistant Legal Adviser of Texaco Trinidad to take up an appointment as a judge on the bench of the Industrial Court of Trinidad and Tobago. The family had another reason to celebrate.

THE MIRACLE

I was the Manager of the Penal branch for sixteen months when the Managing Director again summoned me to his office. He advised that I did an excellent job at Penal and that the Board of Directors had approved my appointment as Manager of the Cipero Street branch, where I would find it more challenging. That branch was close to my home, so I had no problem with that. I was also ready to take on a new challenge.

My husband also received a promotion at the Pointe a Pierre branch as Manager's Assistant, Administration, and this made our children's lives much easier.

Prior to my move to Cipero Street branch, our family spent another holiday in New York at my younger sister who lived there. I had worked at the Cipero Street branch in 1985 during one of my relief stints, and I used to fantasize about taking over management of the branch. It had come true on the 22nd. June 1987. God was working miracles in my life.

The staff worked earnestly to exceed all targets. We received congratulations from the Marketing Department of Head Office for our innovative marketing strategies and for exceeding branch targets. One of our staff members suggested that we hold showcases in the bank's lobby area and courtyard.

We implemented that, and a Trinidad newspaper reported it on the front page of a Trinidad newspaper with a photograph of a showcase as a *'novel idea to stimulate sales.'* Car firms and furniture stores displayed their items in the bank's courtyard and lobby area at varying times. Customers made their selection on the spot and availed of loans to buy the items of their choice. Both bank and businesses benefited.

The branch's business grew because of this strategy, and this pleased my superiors.

When San Fernando became a city, we honoured the first two babies born on 'City Day' at a function hosted by the Cipero Street branch and the Mayor of San Fernando. The Mayor opened two new Savings accounts for the babies as a commemorative gesture on the attainment of city status for San Fernando on November 18th, 1988. This also made the front-page headlines of the same newspapers.

An unfortunate incident took place one afternoon, as my secretary and I were entering the car park at the back of the bank. It was after four o'clock and I had offered her a lift home. As we almost approached my car, a bandit scaled the fence, ran up towards me, and placed a knife to my throat. He demanded cash and a gold chain I was wearing around my neck. I reached into my handbag, and took out the few dollars in there and handed it to him.

When he pointed to the chain around my neck, he said to hurry and hand over the chain.

I burst the chain since I could not undo the clasp. He took the pieces and ran away.

Since we did not get a good look at his face, we did not report the matter to the police.

I advised the Managing Director's Assistant. He told me to erect a barbed wire fence and put in place any security arrangements. It was necessary to prevent a recurrence of such incidents. I took his advice and told my Assistant to proceed.

In the month of May, I received another long service award for twenty-five years of long and dedicated service. The awards function was at the Trinidad Hilton Hotel in Port of Spain. I received a lovely silver tea service.

One of my brothers who was the Acting Comptroller of Customs and Excise in Trinidad and Tobago was in an accident and sustained serious head injuries. He ignored the pains and did not go to see a doctor.

We assumed that everything was all right. One day at work, I decided to call to inquire how he was. His wife answered and said she was happy I called. He complained of feeling unwell and fell down. She felt that something was wrong with him and was taking him to the nursing home. I felt very uncomfortable on hearing that and could not concentrate on my job.

I telephoned my husband in tears and told him we should go to see him that day. He agreed, and he told me to meet him at our home, and he would take me to St. Augustine.

When we arrived in St. Augustine, his daughter, told us they had already left for the nursing home. We drove to the nursing home and found him lying unconscious on a stretcher in the area near to the receptionist. His wife was pleading with the receptionist to admit him but the receptionist told her that the policy of the nursing home was not to admit any patient without a down payment.

She did not walk with any money in her haste to get him medical attention. I realized that it was God who planted the thought in my mind to call to inquire about my brother's health that day. I made the required payment, and they admitted him.

The various doctors did all the tests and told the family they could not operate on his brain since it would be too risky. They advised that they could do nothing more for him and that we should pray. Pray we did, since we believed in prayer.

My other brother asked all of us to hold hands, surround Victor's hospital bed, and join in prayer for his healing. While we were repeating "*The Lord is my shepherd, I shall not want, etc. ....*" my brother awoke from his coma, opened his eyes and joined us in reciting the Psalm. Within a week, he left the nursing home and resumed his normal life. What a miracle that was! We praised God!

My husband and I were finding it difficult to get our vacation at the same time. He got his leave in October 1988 and went to the United Kingdom for a vacation at the home of one of his friends. He had planned to spend four weeks there. His uncle took him to the airport.

I was attending a course at the Bank's Head Office. It was tiring going to Port of Spain every day and returning home to take care of the children's needs. They were young and still attending school.

I missed my husband very much, and when two weeks had passed, I got up from bed at around 5 o'clock one morning and telephoned him. It was 9 o'clock in London. I asked him to cut his holiday short and come home as the children and I missed him. He said it was not possible. He sounded distant and uncaring. I was upset but put the whole thing out of my mind.

At six o'clock that evening, his uncle pulled up in his car in front of our house and asked to see my husband. I told him, "Don't you know he is in London?" My husband got out of the car and, in a feigned accent asked, "When is he coming home?" I did not recognize him in the dark and I answered, "I do not know." He laughed and said, "I am here. I wanted to surprise you."

The children and I were very happy. He explained that he too was missing us and he planned to surprise us by coming home earlier. He did not tell me that when I had called him, as he did not want to spoil the surprise. In fact, when I had called he was dressing to leave London. He brought a suitcase full of beautiful clothes for the children and me. This event stands out in my mind since our feelings were telepathic and it showed how much he cared for his family.

The bank was restructuring its systems into Credit and Operations. The purpose of the course we attended was to show managers the benefits of such a restructuring. All managers had to state their preference for the section of the bank in which they would prefer to work. I selected Credit and my husband selected Operations.

The Board of Directors appointed my husband to Operations Manager of the Penal branch in February 1989. We praised and thanked God with a Thanksgiving service at our home. We never neglected to praise and thank God for his blessings.

I had chosen Credit and there was a surplus of credit managers so I was appointed Relief Credit Manager for South, with effect from 8th May 1989. The job was similar to the Relief Manager position I had earlier on in my career.

The difference was that Credit managers handled a cluster of branches. It entailed more driving when I had to work in clusters with branches that were far apart.

Although the Managing Director told me that I would only have to provide relief in the South, I provided relief in the Port of Spain clusters and even those in the East-West corridor. I loved the job, met many staff and customers, gained experience with lots of business accounts, but the driving was difficult.

To cope with the stress of the job as Relief Credit Manager, I tried to mix business with pleasure. When I worked in the Princes Town/Mayaro/Rio Claro cluster, my husband and I spent weekends in Mayaro with the children and invited the extended family.

My sister-in-law loaned us her beach house and my sisters, brothers, and their families joined us for weekends of fun, sea, and laughter. These family get-togethers helped me to maintain my sanity after driving behind trucks for hours on rocky roads to go to work daily.

I also felt the need to embark upon an extracurricular activity and had an urge to go through my deceased father's diaries and his other records. My brother had earlier mentioned that my father had written about a series of events in his life.

I compiled the book, *'Memoirs of Dr. Andrew Moonir Khan: Journey of an Educator'*. I took many months to do the draft since his handwriting was difficult to read.

I spoke to Sir Isaac Hyatali, T. C.K.B. and he agreed to write the foreword. In August 1989, my husband and I held a book-launching event for that book at our home. I invited all of my father's old friends.

Most of the invited guests attended. I received many praises for my efforts. There were articles in the newspapers about the book and the launching and I kept all the clippings for my scrapbook. Two Presidents in Trinidad and Tobago requested copies of that book, as they both knew my father.

Later in that year, my husband and I took our children to Caracas for a vacation. One of my sisters, Sybil, and her husband accompanied us on that trip. We stayed at the magnificent Anauco Hilton Hotel. We all went shopping on Saturday after we arrived.

Somehow, we split up, and my husband and my sister's husband disappeared. We retraced our steps to find them, but in vain. After we searched and searched for hours with no success, we returned to the hotel to inquire if they had gone back there. The hotel receptionist said he did not see them, and no one requested keys for our rooms.

We went to our room and prayed for their safe return. We had heard that people were kidnapped in strange countries and we were fearful that our husbands might have met a similar fate.

Unexpectedly they appeared. They said they too were searching for us and worried if anyone had kidnapped us. We thanked God that we were together again.

27th July 1990 and the week that followed was another most traumatic period in our lives. Muslim terrorists stormed the Red House and took over the only television station in Trinidad. The perpetrators took our Prime Minister and other ministers as hostages.

They shot the Prime Minister in his leg and killed a Government minister.

Our country remained at a standstill while negotiations took place to arrive at a settlement for their demands.

Rumours of violence and looting circulated. Police stations and other buildings were burnt to the ground. Businesses and schools remained closed and the President declared a state of emergency. Banks remained closed. When it was all resolved, the banks opened its doors on a Sunday to facilitate customers who needed money.

That morning there was a stampede in the bank when the bank in which I was working opened.

Customers were desperate to complete financial transactions and go back home. Their feet, as they rushed into the bank, sounded like horses galloping. It was a not a nice period in our lives.

My husband and I took the children to Margarita for a vacation. Margarita, part of Venezuela, lies in the Caribbean Sea about 40 kilometers north of the mainland. It's a popular holiday destination.

In Margarita, we felt free. We could have walked the streets at any hour without fear. We still had nightmares while we were on holiday and dreaded returning home. It took many months for people on the island to regain a sense of security.

JEALOUS MISCHIEF MAKER

As both my husband and I had attained management positions in the bank, this incurred jealousy in the minds of co-workers who we thought were our friends.

When my husband was just 43 years old, he had to resign from his job at the bank because an envious co-worker tried to make mischief. He accused my husband of something he did not do, and the bank authorities listened to the co-worker's accusations instead of my husband.

My son had just completed his Advanced Levels, and my daughter had just passed her C.X.C. examinations. They were ready to further their studies and needed lots of funding to do so.

The University of the West Indies in Barbados had accepted my son to pursue a degree in Computer Science.

My daughter gained acceptance into a Canadian School in Toronto for Grade 13. My son had to turn down his offer of acceptance for the Barbados University to pursue a different course at the University of the West Indies, St. Augustine.

Luckily, we had friends in Toronto who assisted my daughter with a place to stay for a while. My niece, who also lived in Toronto, accommodated her for part of the school year. I had to make several adjustments in my life to finance their education while my husband remained unemployed. Before we had received the news of my husband's forced resignation from the bank, my eldest sister, Myrtle, and I had booked a flight to go to Miami to buy warm clothing for my daughter to take to Toronto. My husband told us to go ahead with our plans, and we did so.

He could not find another job for quite a few months and was depressed. He made an attempt at business by going into partnership with a friend. He used most of his savings in that venture, but it did not work out. His father passed away in November of that year, and that further depressed him. His sister's brother-in-law gave him a job as a Credit Manager at his business place, but for a short time only. The business closed after a few months.

After a few more months of unsuccessful applications to other firms, he got a job with similar benefits to the one he had at the bank. He began his tenure with the company as Credit Manager, and after Central Bank introduced new guidelines, they added the portfolio of Anti-Money Laundering Compliance Officer to his position as Credit Manager. He held that job until his retirement in March 2014.

I must admit it was difficult for me to continue working in the bank after my husband left. Although I wanted to resign from my job as well, we needed the income. Therefore, I continued working and gave of my best.

Being a forgiving person, I remained friends with those who tried to bring down my husband.

One day at a meeting in Head Office, a Director saw me laughing and chatting with someone. He called me aside and told me, "Brenda, I can see you are a real Christian." He was right. I always leave judgment to God.

The Manager who took over my husband's job told us he did a full investigation and found no truth in the allegations against my husband. He also found out that the one who caused the mischief was hoping to get my husband's job, but he never did. He retired without getting further promotions.

That experience made both my husband and me into much stronger individuals and brought us much closer to God.

When my daughter completed her course of studies in Toronto, my son and I went to Toronto for a short vacation, to help her bring home her luggage.

My youngest sister and her family were holidaying in Toronto at the same time we were there. They were visiting a relative who lived in Toronto. They picked us up and took us to their stately home in Markham, where they were having a family gathering. We went shopping together at the Eaton's Centre. Other relatives came to visit us at my daughter's apartment. They took us to visit the famous Niagara Falls. The sheer beauty of the waterfall astounded us once more.

My son always had a love for Computer Studies, and both he and my daughter pursued external degrees in Computing and Information Systems from the University of London since we could not afford to send them abroad. Their degrees are recognized worldwide and they hold top jobs today.

In 1992, the Regional Credit Manager in Head Office in Port of Spain asked Management to assign me to his office. He required me to help him with sundry duties.

He told me he was impressed with the way I handled the assignments, and he made me feel a sense of achievement each time he praised me for a job well done. Thereafter, I felt that my career was moving forward once more.

On 7th October 1993, we celebrated my son's birthday at our home. It was a small celebration, but everyone attending had fun. It was a surprise party, and he was surprised. He stuck the birthday cake with his girlfriend whom he knew from school days.

In November 1993, the President of Trinidad and Tobago appointed my brother as Vice-President of the Industrial Court of Trinidad and Tobago. It was a prestigious appointment and well deserved. The family rejoiced with him.

In March 1994, my son was visiting his girlfriend at her home.

His finger got caught in the electronic gate and was almost severed. The doctor told him he might lose the finger. The next day when I went to work at the High Street branch, I told a friend who was well- known for her prayer sessions in the Bank. She had prayed with many staff members and their problems were solved. Jenny Radhay prayed with me in my office for my son's finger. Every night the family continued to pray at home with my son for his healing. The finger healed miraculously. God had once more answered our prayers.

UPWARD CAREER MOVES

On 7th April 1994, the Board of Directors of the Bank appointed me as Assistant Area Credit Manager of the High Street cluster, which comprised of four branches - High Street, Harris Promenade, Cipero Street, and Pointe a Pierre. The Regional Credit Manager recommended my appointment and told me he had every confidence that I would do a good job.

In April 1995, my elder sister was elevated to Principal of the Vistabella Presbyterian School after acting for two years on the job. All the brothers and sisters in my family had responsible jobs in the country.

As Assistant Area Manager of the High Street cluster of the bank, I was again working close to my home. I had worked as Relief Credit Manager in that cluster on some occasions and it did not take me long to settle down on the job.

I felt comfortable working with both the Senior Area Credit Manager and the Area Credit Manager. The staff members of all four branches were cooperative. My job as Assistant Area Credit Manager entailed dealing with personal loans to customers. I found that was not enough for someone with my experience. I grabbed every opportunity I had, to help the other managers in handling as many commercial loans as possible.

In my job, I had responsibility for staff matters and for the financial plan for the four branches. The staff under my control worked to achieve the targets set and at the end of the financial year, the actual figures exceeded all targets for both Personal and Commercial Lendings

I received an excellent staff report from my superiors and in January 1996, the Board appointed me to Area Credit Manager of the High Street cluster.

My son took a part-time job at the Harris Promenade branch of the Bank in February 1996. He wanted to work and study part-time to complete his degree. He received a promotion one year later to the Management Services Department of the bank in Port of Spain. That was a position I was offered when I was pregnant with him.

That year, the hand of God intervened once more in my son's life. He was driving home after classes late one evening, when the car he was driving skidded off the wet road, somersaulted quite a few times, and landed on its hood in the northbound lane.

The car was a write-off, yet my son walked away without one hair of his head harmed. God is great. My sister-in-law arranged for the church leaders of the Marabella Presbyterian church to hold a small thanksgiving service at our home to praise and thank God for his everlasting kindness to my family.

My daughter also took a job as a part-time cashier in the High Street branch of the Bank in the final year of her studies for her degree. This helped her to have pocket change and to buy clothing. This relieved my husband and me of part of the financial burden.

During my tenure as Area Credit Manager of the High Street cluster, I acted as Senior Area Credit Manager a few times. I enjoyed my job and the relationships I shared with the staff and customers. I also enjoyed co-hosting the lavish annual customer Christmas cocktail parties, which the High Street branch organized.

Staff members of all four branches were eager to exceed the targets set for business growth and profitability, and we did so consistently. The cluster earned an enviable reputation in the organization.

In December 1996, my son became engaged to his girlfriend, Chitra, from his school days.

The Reverend Cyril Paul (since deceased) officiated at the ceremony at our home.

In January 1997, the Bank appointed me as one of the Bank's attorneys to execute legal documents arising in the ordinary course of business of the Bank. That was an indication of the faith and trust which my employers placed in me.

In May of that year, I received another award from the Bank's Management. At the Long Service Awards ceremony at the Trinidad Hilton Hotel, the Managing Director presented me with a Cash voucher for 35 years of long and faithful service.

On the 8th. July 1997, my eldest sister's husband passed away after a long illness. I felt as if I had lost a brother. It was a traumatic experience for my sister, but she was fortunate to have her seven devoted children and her loving brothers and sisters at her side to comfort her.

We experienced another family trauma in early August. Our daughter got in a car accident driving home after work at the bank. She suffered bruises and whiplash and two weeks later, she had to undergo emergency surgery.

Our fervent prayers helped her to make a speedy recovery. On 23rd. August 1997, our son married his fiancé in an elegant wedding ceremony at the Susamachar Presbyterian Church.

My sister, Rose, came from London for the occasion. Preparing and shopping for the event was a great deal of fun and added spice to my life.

I enjoyed writing and sending out the invitations, selecting the venue and collaborating with the decorator for both church and reception. My sisters and my nieces helped me to prepare the cake boxes, on which the names of the bride and groom were imprinted. My eldest sister baked the delicious black cake to put in the boxes. We also wrapped chocolates in sparkling tinsel paper for the children.

When the day came I felt satisfied that everything turned out the way we planned. Our daughter-in-law was a gorgeous bride. Her bridesmaids, including our daughter who had recovered by that time, all looked beautiful.

Our son was a handsome groom, and the best man and groomsmen all looked sharp. The decorators did a fabulous job, and both bride and groom were pleased.

Both Reverend Joy Abdul and Reverend Cyril Paul (deceased) officiated at the church ceremony. A lavish reception with about three hundred and fifty guests followed at the Gulf City Auditorium.

Guests enjoyed live entertainment by a dance troupe. Everyone who attended that wedding remarked on how well organized and entertaining they found it to be. They also commented on the lovely floral table decorations, which they helped themselves to after the reception.

When the formalities were over and the delicious meal consumed, guests danced until the wee hours of the morning.

A week after the wedding, both our son and daughter received the results of their final examinations. They both attained Bachelor of Science degrees with honours in Computing and Information Systems from the University of London External Degree program. The School of Accounting and Management held a grand graduation ceremony at the Trinidad Hilton Hotel Ballroom. My husband and I felt proud to have both our children graduate with degrees.

Our daughter-in-law completed the Diploma in the local Banking Examinations two months later, and this also made us proud. Once again, we had cause to praise and thank God for his wonderful grace and blessings.

SAD MOMENTS

The year 1998 started brightly for our family. Both my children resigned from Republic Bank in December 1997 and took jobs more in line with their qualifications. My son and daughter-in-law got approval for their house plans to build their home, and everyone's future seemed bright.

We held a Thanksgiving service at our home to give thanks and glory to God. Reverend Joy Abdul officiated at the service. In her sermon, she drew reference to the fact that our family recognized that God gave our talents, and our successes were because of our use of those talents. It was fitting to give God the Glory. Then the sad news came a few days later. My sister Sybil, who was not well since she fell down in the car park after my son's wedding, learned from her doctor she had a critical illness.

190

She was suffering from chronic renal failure and had less than twelve months to live. This news threw a dark shadow over our lives.

My sister from London took a flight to Trinidad when she heard the news. She spent three weeks with us, and we all visited our sick sister often and prayed for her healing.

Once again, the Bank saw the need to restructure its operations because of the rapid growth in business. They renamed Area Credit Managers as Commercial Credit Managers who had responsibility for only Commercial Lendings. My job was, therefore, Commercial Credit Manager, San Fernando Commercial Credit Centre.

The San Fernando Commercial Credit Centre was temporarily located in Gulf City Mall. The High Street branch, which was to house the Commercial Credit Centre, had to be re-built.

My daughter started a job as an Information Technology officer at a popular firm and they sent her to St. Maarten to handle the Computer Operations on that island. The jobholder in that island had tendered his resignation to return to his home in another island. She loved it there until Hurricane George stormed through the Caribbean with rage and fury, leaving several small islanders dead or homeless.

She had checked into a hotel before the hurricane arrived in St. Maarten. Although only the tail end of the hurricane hit the island, her apartment on the sea suffered damage, leaving her without water and lights for several days. Both my husband and I thanked God for keeping our daughter safe.

On 30th September 1998 she returned home to work in the Trinidad office of the firm. She later announced her plans to marry someone she met in St. Maarten.

He was the person from whom she took over the job. He came to Trinidad in November to ask for her hand in marriage and we gave them our blessings. The date for the wedding was 24th. April 1999. The ceremony was to take place at the Susamachar Presbyterian Church and the reception at the Petrotrin Staff Club. It was a thrill to plan a second wedding in the family.

My husband also received exciting news from the bank. The Managing Director advised that the bank was willing to settle the outstanding court matter, which my husband had filed against them for forced resignation in 1991. A settlement figure was agreed.

April 24th arrived before we knew it. Michelle was a radiant bride. Everyone said she looked like a princess with her simple, yet beautiful wedding gown and glittering tiara. The wedding started on time and everything went smoothly. Michelle's husband's relatives came from Guadeloupe, Paris, and the United States for the wedding.

The chief bridesmaid took time off from her studies in Toronto to be present for the joyous occasion.

All the bridesmaids looked striking in their midnight blue gowns. The decorators did a marvelous job of decorating the church and club in blue, silver and white. Musicians played terrific music for dancing. Caterers served sumptuous meals, hors d'oeuvres, desserts, and a variety of drinks. Michelle had an amazing wedding cake. It was nine-tiered and decorated with fresh red roses.

A groomsman spoke in French on the bridegroom's behalf and another Guadeloupian translated it for the audience. There were two hundred and twenty-five people present and they all said they had an enjoyable time.

My sister, Sybil, who was ill could not attend because of her deteriorating condition. My oldest brother, Gilbert, was also not well and could not attend. I was very disappointed that they could not have joined us on such a joyous occasion.

There is a sad ending to this chapter of my life. On 3rd, June 1999, which was a public holiday, Sybil telephoned me at home. She told me she wanted to see all of her sisters and brothers at her home. My sister-in-law had already made arrangements with me and the other sisters to visit her on that day, and I told her we would be there.

Our brother, Addison, accompanied us, and upon our arrival, we met our oldest brother, Gilbert, and his wife, Helen, who had arrived there earlier. Sybil was delighted to see us. She had picked many fruits from her garden to share with us. She told us she was going to India for treatment the following day and would be back in three weeks. Little did we realize that was the last time we would see her.

We bade her farewell and prayed that she would return home cured. She left with her husband, Alfred, and younger son, David, on 4th June 1999. During their stay abroad, we did not receive much news about her condition, but the brief messages received from her elder son, Peter, by our older brother indicated that her health was improving.

On 8th, July 1999, it was with shock and dismay we received news that Sybil had passed away on the flight back home while the plane was circling over Heathrow London airport. When my older brother telephoned me at the bank to tell me of her death, it sounded unbelievable, and the tears flowed swiftly. I felt as if I was in a daze. My secretary was most understanding. She advised the other managers and staff. They came to comfort me and offer their sympathy. My secretary assisted me in clearing my desk and making phone calls to my husband and children.

Her husband decided to cremate her body and conduct the funeral rites in London. Myrtle was holidaying at my other sister, Rose, who lives in London, and they both attended the last rites over there. Our youngest sister and her daughter travelled from Los Angeles to Trinidad for a vacation.

They had hoped to meet my sister while she was still alive and were very disappointed.

Addison and his wife held several touching prayer services with all the entire family at their home to remember our dear sister.

A friend of my deceased sister, Roma Sinanan, composed a heart-rending poem about their friendship, which began in childhood days. She broke down while reading it. Another friend told us of a conversation she had with my sister some time ago.

She said a few friends were discussing their problems with my sister, and she gave this advice. *'Sometimes in life, there will not always be chocolates and ice cream. If life hands you a lemon, use it to make lemonade.'*

The family held a memorial service at the Curepe Presbyterian Church on 23rd July 1999 the date of my beloved sister's birthday. Reverend Daniel Teelucksingh officiated.

The church was packed. All her friends from the Inner Wheel Club, the women's arm of the Rotary Club, of which she was a Past President, and the Rotary Club of St. Augustine, of which her husband was a Past President, were present.

All her close acquaintances also attended. Her son read the Eulogy, and Florabelle read a Tribute in her honour. The remaining sisters sang a song, 'Our hearts will go on.' A brave little niece composed a song about her, and she sang it at the service.

My sister's passing away left a void in the hearts of her husband, sons, and each of her brothers and sisters, who loved her very much. One wonderful sister and friend, who, despite her illness, was always so very cheerful, left us. She was the fifth in the family and was sixty years old when she returned to her Maker. She was the sister I used to call "Billy" when I was a little girl. We accepted the will of God and are comforted by these words of Mother Teresa: 'DEATH IS NOTHING ELSE BUT GOING HOME TO GOD; THE BOND OF LOVE WILL BE UNBROKEN FOR ALL ETERNITY.'

A BROTHER DIES

My sister's death made me realize that our lives are short and we need to do all we can to make life worth living for ourselves and those around us.

We received good news and more bad news before 1999 ended. My oldest brother, Gilbert, died. He died the day after the President of Trinidad and Tobago appointed my third brother. Addison, as President of the Industrial Court of Trinidad and Tobago.

After my sister's death, Gilbert was heart-broken and fell ill. He never recovered. On the day he died, he telephoned every one of his brothers and sisters to wish them all the best. When he called my home, both my husband and I spoke to him. He said although he had emergency dialysis the night before he still was not feeling well.

He inquired about the children and wished them happiness. We suspected from the tone of his voice that he was saying farewell to us. It was very painful to lose another sibling so soon after our sister died.

In August 1999, I fell ill with the flu. My doctor suspected that I had dengue fever and he hospitalized me in the Victoria Nursing Home for three days. He gave me medication and three bags of drips. The tests proved negative for dengue fever. I was weak and had to stay away from work on sick leave for two weeks. When the doctor discharged me from the nursing home, my husband fell ill and he too spent three days in the nursing home.

During the period of my illness, I felt myself drawn much closer to God and felt a deep urge to read the Bible daily. I felt I needed a deeper understanding of him and felt satisfied with my progress in that respect with each passing day.

When I returned to work, I saw everything and everyone in a new light.

I knew I would soon reach the compulsory retirement age of 55 years for women in the Bank and had to accept it. I did not look forward to it. I was still young and wanted to continue working. There was talk about bringing the retirement age for women in line with men, but up to that time, nothing happened to increase it.

I observed members of the staff holding secret meetings often and they stopped speaking whenever I passed their way. I suspected that they were planning my retirement party. One day my secretary and my assistant approached me to tell me of the plans. They requested the names of my relatives whom I wanted to be present at the retirement function, which they planned for September 25th, 1999, the day I was proceeding on pre-retirement leave.

Customers and staff members treated me to many lunches during that time, and everyone had wonderful things to say about me. Many said they wished I would not leave.

Others praised me for turning them into millionaires. The following week I handed over my portfolio of accounts to the manager appointed by the Board of the bank to take over my position.

On my last day at work, the staff of the San Fernando Commercial Credit Centre had a luncheon to bid me goodbye. They presented me with a lovely hand band and told me to wear it to the retirement party at Soong's Great Wall Restaurant on September 25th.

On that same day, the Deputy Managing Director telephoned me at work and told me to call at his office for an exit interview. My son-in-law, Raphael, drove me to Port of Spain for the meeting. Mr. Huggins and I had a very interesting discussion. He told me I had a long, interesting, varied, and successful career of which I should be very proud. I should feel fulfilled and should think before committing myself to any full-time job again.

I respected the Deputy Managing Director very much and considered his advice worthwhile. However, I was still young and I intended to work again whether it was full- time or part- time. My children were all grown up and married and my husband was still working. I needed to find an avenue to make use of my skills and to continue to make a difference in the lives of others.

One episode of my life was over and I was about to begin a new chapter, the events of which may or may not fill many pages. My advice to everyone is brief. Fill your mind with positive thoughts, pray for wisdom to achieve your goals, and "Do your best and God will do the rest."

MY RETIREMENT PARTY

I can only describe the retirement party as an enchanting evening. When I entered the exquisitely decorated restaurant with my husband, Nishazad Nagir, an ex-staff member, presented me with a bouquet of yellow and white roses. Aleem Cassim took my hand and led me to the Head table. On my way, all the guests stood up to hug and kiss me.

Aleem was the Master of Ceremonies. The Board of the Bank had appointed him as a Manager of a branch in Central Trinidad. He worked with me when I was Manager of the Cipero Street branch, and I found him a promising young man. I always told him he would be a manager one day, and he lived up to my recommendations and expectation.

Reverend Cyril Paul [now deceased], my church minister, was present to say the opening prayer.

Mr. Ronald Huggins, Deputy Managing Director of the Bank, who gave the feature address on behalf of the Bank, was next.

Mr. Huggins disclosed many well-kept secrets in his speech. In his opening remarks, he stated that he considered it an honour to speak at my retirement party. When he thought of Brenda Mohammed, he thought of me as one of the female pioneers of the Bank.

I was one of the first women to write and succeed in the Institute of Bankers examinations, and at an early stage in my career, I developed a reputation as one who would move forward in the bank. He recalled when my name changed by marriage from Brenda Khan to Brenda Mohammed. From there, he went on to outline my various promotions.

He advised that he was the one who recommended me as sub-manager of the Penal branch and had no regrets in doing so. When the Managing Director of the Bank asked him to recommend someone to set up the Corporate Division South, he could think of no one else with the technical expertise but Brenda Mohammed. He thanked me for giving him yeoman support when the Board of Directors transferred him to Corporate Division South as the Senior Corporate Manager.

During that time, I was his right-hand person. He revealed that he recommended my upgrading to managerial status and felt that in an era when mostly males were board-appointed officials that I was a pioneering female for the Board of Directors to appoint me as a manager. Showering praises on me for my job performance and acknowledging my contributions and achievements throughout the years, he thanked me for my faithful years of service and commitment to the Bank.

Mr. Brian Samlalsingh was the guest speaker and he too showered praises and more or less confirmed what Mr. Huggins said. He added that another of my major accomplishments was building up the Penal sub-branch to full branch status within twelve months. He said it was interesting to note that not only did I excel in my job, but I also had other talents such as writing and singing.

During the open session, many staff members, fellow managers, and customers made speeches and said many complimentary things about me. My husband Rashiff shocked everyone when he got up and said remarkable things about me from a speech he had prepared without my knowledge.

Aleem Cassim stated that I was his mentor and responsible for his success in the bank. Customers said that with my knowledge and assistance, and the bank's finance, their businesses turned into profitable enterprises.

The kind words of everyone brought tears to my eyes, and I had to compose myself before I replied.

My sister, Florabelle, gave the vote of thanks, just as the organizing committee had asked her to do.

The dinner was sumptuous and a singer entertained us while we dined.

When I opened my gifts, I realized why the staff wanted me to wear the hand band they had given me the evening before the party. It matched with the exquisite Accurist watch they presented me that night.

I also received a diamond and sapphire necklace with matching earrings, a keepsake journal of good wishes, and a huge basket of dried flowers. It was an unforgettable event and I happy to see members of my family, dearest friends, customers, staff, and top officials of the bank present.

A copy of the video tape recording of the retirement party was given to me a few weeks after the event.

EPILOGUE

This is not the end of my story. My story continues in my next book, *"Retirement is Fun: When one door closes, another opens."*

I have seen the Bank evolve from manual and primitive operations in post-office-like structures to computerized systems in magnificent buildings all over the island. The customer base changed from illiterate and semi-illiterate to a very educated and knowledgeable clientele. I consider myself fortunate to have been part of this organization, survived the many changes, and to have served in the leading and most indigenous Bank in the Caribbean.

It is thrilling to recall moments in the bank such as when a new judge received his first pay cheque payable to 'His Honour Mr..........'..The excitement on his face and his expression when he brought the cheque to deposit into his account are unforgettable. He said, "Imagine a cheque made out as 'His Honour.' My wife and kids were thrilled."

My memory flashes back to my first interview with the proprietor of a funeral home who wanted to set up the first crematorium in the island.

"How is business?" I inquired.

"Dead," he remarked.

Incidentally, that conversation inspired me to write a short story, 'Dead Business.' It is one of the short stories in Heart-Warming Tales, one of my publications.

Another man came to see me by appointment. He wanted a loan. His first words were, "I am a million dollars short of being a millionaire."

I remember a very nice illiterate lady who came to the bank once a week to withdraw her money, take it home, count it, to make sure it was all there, and return to re-deposit it the following day.

I enjoyed working at the bank and I want to acknowledge those persons who contributed to my successful career:

Mr. Wright, for employing me [everyone said he was right to do so.], Mr. Wilbert Smith, Mr. Sam Seupersad, Mr. William Balfour, Mr. Christopher Gunby, Mr. Adrian Bird, Mr. Ronald Huggins, Mr. Ronald Harford, Mr. Robert Norstrom, Mr. Azad Mohammed, Mr. Ken O'Reilly, Mr. Brian Samlalsingh, Mr. Lester Moore, and many others too numerous to mention. Most of all I must acknowledge all the loyal staff members who worked with me at the various branches throughout the island. Without their support, I could not have succeeded.

Most importantly, I thank my husband, children, parents, and siblings, for their love and support.

There is a saying, "If your life is worth living, it is worth recording." Mine was worth living.

What was my life like after my retirement from the Bank?

Read the sequel.

Retirement is Fun: When one door closes another opens.

RETIREMENT IS FUN

WHEN ONE DOOR CLOSES, MANY OTHERS OPEN.

In her memoir RETIREMENT IS FUN, which is a sequel to My Life as a Banker - A Life Worth Living, Brenda describes her many wonderful experiences at the end of her banking career.

Reluctant to move on from banking, she amazes herself when she turned down an offer to work in a higher position at another bank.

She chose Insurance instead, and for her, it turned out to be the better choice.

She excelled and qualified for the Premium Association for Financial Professionals [MDRT] six times in a row and her travels around the world skyrocketed.

Within the pages. you will read how Brenda proves that retirement is a time to enjoy life and continue to earn. For her, retirement is when you stop working to live, and start working at living.

Of course, life is not a bed of roses, and you will read how Brenda stands out as a beacon of light throughout every challenge she faces.

Follow the author on her remarkable journey.

Read a five-star review from an Amazon Reviewer:

"Great Motivational Read!

What can I say about "Retirement Is Fun?" It's a book that gives the good and the bad of living in this 21st century. There are incredible miracles and incredible heartbreaks, yet through it all with the support of family and faith in God, we prevail.

The author wrote the story as it occurred, with no frills or embellishments. She takes the reader along with her to the many places she visited. Her obvious enjoyment in them is a testament to her wonderful spirit.

The book is written in two parts. I was happy the author gives us the good news in the first half, that way, the reader is able to see her strength and appreciate from whence she came. I was impressed with the places she had visited. I'd thought I was a world traveler, but I take my hat off to her and her wonderful family.

This is a great motivational and inspirational story for anyone who needs uplifting."

AUTHOR'S BIOGRAPHY

Brenda Mohammed is a prolific, multi-award-winning author from Trinidad and Tobago, with 67 published books spanning science fiction, memoir, mystery, romance, poetry, and more. Her gripping sci-fi saga Zeeka Chronicles has been adapted into a five-part screenplay, primed for film or television.

Her horror screenplay, Zeeka and the Zombies, has earned the distinction of becoming a finalist in the 13Horror.com Screenplay Contest 2025.

Before her literary ascent, Brenda was a trailblazer in banking and insurance, rising to senior leadership at Republic Bank Limited and earning international recognition as a top-tier financial professional. Her career helped shape communities and drive economic growth across Trinidad and Tobago.

She later excelled in insurance, earning the prestigious Million Dollar Round Table qualification six times and a Life Underwriting Fellowship from the American College, USA.

Her writing journey began after surviving a near-fatal battle with cancer. That experience birthed 'I Am Cancer Free,' a bestselling memoir that won global acclaim. Brenda's works have since earned honours across five continents—including the PLATO Award, Socrates Award, and Dante Alighieri Award from CIESART Spain, Reader's Favorite International Awards (USA), Author Academy Award, Literary Global Award, and the CLR Award (India).

Founder of the How to Write for Success Literary Network, Brenda has mentored countless writers and published anthologies and magazines that uplift voices worldwide. Her self-help guide 'How to Write for Success' was hailed by the Ethiopian Herald as "a comprehensive toolkit for writers, critics, and editors."

A Peace Ambassador and advocate against domestic violence, human trafficking, drug addiction, and suicide, Brenda's influence extends beyond the page.

She's a member of Stage 32, connecting her to the global film and TV community, and continues to inspire through humanitarian work, literary leadership, and cinematic storytelling.

In a world where stories shape lives, Brenda Mohammed emerges as a beacon—her words healing wounds, building communities, and transforming the literary landscape from Trinidad and Tobago to the world stage.

Brenda Mohammed inspires and challenges readers worldwide with her impactful works.

A Remarkable Literary Journey

Her catalogue showcases not only her immense talent but also her deep commitment to addressing both personal and global challenges through storytelling. Below is a curated overview of her diverse and impactful body of work.

Children's Books: Nurturing Young Minds and Hearts

Brenda's children's books introduce young readers to the world through heart-warming and imaginative stories that captivate the imagination while imparting valuable lessons.

Adventures of Squeaky Doo (2014) takes readers on the travel memoirs of a beloved teddy bear, sharing the wonder of discovery.

She Cried for Me (2017) offers a poignant autobiography from the perspective of a stray dog, combining empathy with an important message about compassion.

The Child Poet (2020) brings poetry to children, inviting them into a poetic galaxy full of wonder and creativity. This book became a hot release upon publication, delighting young minds with verse.

Psychological Thrillers: Unravelling Minds and Mysteries

Brenda's psychological thrillers are gripping, fast-paced, and designed to keep readers on the edge of their seats. Her ability to weave suspense with character complexity makes her a standout in the genre.

The Manipulator (2021) delves deep into the mind of a manipulative figure, leaving readers questioning trust and human behaviour.

Conspiracy Stories (2021) features three chilling tales that awaken the mind and explore the dark side of human nature.

Mystery Thrillers – Barry Holmes Series: Crime, Suspense, and Romance

The Barry Holmes Series, a mix of crime fiction and romance, is one of Brenda's most popular works, capturing the intrigue and mystery of disappearances and unsolved crimes.

The Gift of Love (2018) mixes crime fiction with romance, engaging readers in a plot that keeps them guessing.

The Axe Murderer (2019) takes on kidnapping and suspense, blending shocking twists with emotional depth.

What Happened to Mary Loo (2020) explores the mystery of a post-lockdown disappearance.

Tales of Mysterious Disappearances (2020) brings together three mind-bending mysteries that leave readers questioning the truth.

Memoirs: Sharing Stories of Life and Resilience

Brenda's memoirs offer an intimate look at her life and the experiences that have shaped her. These stories of resilience, family, and career offer inspiration and reflection.

I Am Cancer Free (2013) recounts her miraculous recovery from cancer, offering hope and strength to others facing illness.

Memoirs of Dr. A. M. Khan (2014) sheds light on her father's life during the Indentureship in Trinidad and Tobago, revealing a deeply personal family history.

My Life as a Banker (2014) chronicles Brenda's journey through the banking sector, offering motivational insights into the world of business.

Retirement is Fun (2014) captures the adventures and joys of life after her banking career, showcasing her ability to find fulfilment in new chapters.

Travel Memoirs with Pictures (2014) presents a visual journey around the world, blending storytelling with the beauty of photography.

Christian Books: Faith, Inspiration, and Wisdom

Blending poetic inspiration with biblical teachings, Brenda's Christian books speak to the heart, providing spiritual guidance and encouragement.

Titles like Your Time Is Now, He is the One, Chosen by the Creator, and Serenity in End Times (2014–2024) offer uplifting messages and biblical wisdom to help readers navigate life's challenges.

True Power of Love, God-Fearing Ones, Christmas Messages, and Now is the Time encourage faith-driven living, while Keys to Withstanding Storms of

Life offers practical advice to find strength in times of hardship.

Poetry Collections: Reflections of the Soul

Brenda's poetry collections have touched readers' hearts by addressing universal themes of love, resilience, and identity.

Collections like Strength for the Disheartened, Dreams of the Heart, and A Road Travelled (2019–2024) explore emotions ranging from loss to joy.

Chaotic Times and Sweet Medley capture the complexities of life, while Just for You and Treasured Memories celebrate love and personal reflection. Save God's Earth: Poems on Climate Change, Peace, Love, and Humanity is a call for a stop to the earth's pollution and injustices.

Romance: Heartfelt and Endearing Tales

Brenda's romance novels capture the beauty and complexity of relationships with heart-warming and tender narratives.

Stories People Love (2014) and Heart-Warming Tales (2014) explore themes of love, connection, and the magic of romance.

Stories that Intrigue (2019) presents a unique love story between two writers, blending creativity and passion.

Science Fiction – Revenge of Zeeka Series: A Futuristic Saga

Brenda's Zeeka Chronicles is a science fiction series that combines thrilling narratives with futuristic elements, such as zombies, robots, and human resilience.

Titles like Zeeka and the Zombies (2016), Zeeka and the Zombies II [2025], and Zeeka's Ghost (2017) create a post-apocalyptic world where survival and courage are paramount.

Resurrection and the award-winning Zeeka Chronicles (2016–2017)

complete the saga, which was also adapted into a five-part screenplay, reaching new heights in the world of sci-fi.

The Zeeka Chronicles is a remarkable contribution to the genre, mixing imagination with powerful themes of survival and human spirit.

Most recently, her screenplay, Zeeka and the Zombies, has earned the distinction of becoming a finalist in the 13Horror.com Screenplay Contest 2025, further solidifying its place as a groundbreaking work in both literature and visual media. This recognition marks a significant step for Brenda as her stories leap off the pages and into the realm of film and television.

Self-Help & Writing Guides: Empowering the Next Generation of Writers

Through her self-help books, Brenda shares invaluable knowledge and experience with aspiring authors.

How to Write for Success (2017, 2021) and Self-Publishing Tips (2022) provide practical advice for budding authors, helping them navigate the complexities of the writing and publishing world.

Poetry Anthologies and Magazines: Amplifying Voices for Change

Brenda has also edited and co-authored poetry anthologies that address vital social issues.

A Spark of Hope (2019–2023) and Break the Silence (2020–2025) tackle topics such as suicide prevention, domestic violence, human trafficking, and addiction.

Peace Begins with Us (2022) and Creating a Better World (2022) encourage readers to take action for positive change.

A Literary Legacy That Endures

Brenda Mohammed's literary catalogue is a testament to the power of words, creativity, and resilience. Explore

Brenda's full catalogue of works, and discover how her stories can enrich your life. Visit her Amazon Author Page and follow her on social media to stay connected with her latest releases and literary endeavours.

COPYRIGHT NOTICE